I0154374

NEVER LOST

The Black Church as God's Ark of the Covenant

W. FRANKLYN RICHARDSON

WHARTON CURTIS PRESS

AN IMPRINT OF THE CHURCH ONLINE, LLC

*Many books have been written about the Black Church,
but this book is from the Black Church.*

–Dr. W. Franklyn Richardson

Copyright © 2025 by W. Franklyn Richardson

All rights reserved. No part of this book may be reproduced, stored in a retrieval system, or transmitted in any form or by any means—electronic, mechanical, photocopying, recording, or otherwise—without prior written permission from the publisher, except for brief quotations used in critical reviews or articles.

Published by:

Wharton Curtis Press
An Imprint of The Church Online, LLC
P.O. Box 209
Forbes Road, PA 15633
Phone: 412-349-0049

Scripture Acknowledgements

Scripture quotations are taken from the following versions:
The Holy Bible, King James Version (KJV). Public domain.

The Holy Bible, New King James Version® (NKJV).
Copyright © 1982 by Thomas Nelson. All rights reserved.

Disclaimer

The views and opinions expressed in this book are those of the author and do not necessarily reflect the official policy or position of the publisher. Every effort has been made to ensure the accuracy of the information presented in this book; however, the publisher assumes no responsibility for errors or omissions.

ISBN: 978-1-68548-030-1

Library of Congress Control Number: 2025917784

Printed in the United States of America.

First Edition: 2026

For inquiries about this book, please contact the publisher.

Advance Praise

Our churches, our colleges, our fraternities, our businesses all started in the Black Church. There's no one more respected and renowned to interpret the Black Church and its legacy than Rev. Dr. W. Franklyn Richardson. This book is not suggested reading; it's mandatory.

Reverend Al Sharpton
Founder and President, National Action Network

Dr. W. Franklyn Richardson has long been a pillar in my life and in the Black community. In *Never Lost*, he embodies the moral leadership generations have turned to for guidance and inspiration. His universal messages resonate deeply with me and will continue to be a compass for future leaders seeking wisdom inspired by faith and cultural tradition.

Robert Smith
Founder, Chair, and CEO, Vista Equity Partners Management, LLC

Dedication

This book is dedicated to the people of Grace Baptist Church in Mount Vernon, NY, who have loved me for fifty years and whom I have loved.

Gratitude

I am deeply indebted to the Conference of National Black Churches (CNBC) community, especially the many attendees who reviewed the pre-publication manuscript and offered invaluable insights. Under the guidance of the national leadership of each CNBC member denomination, their critiques have helped shape the work you now hold.

I am also profoundly grateful to my dear colleague and friend, Dr. Ralph Douglas West, a celebrated and trusted voice of the Church, for graciously penning the foreword.

This book is offered as a contribution to the ongoing critique of the Black Church, written in the hope that this vital institution will continue to serve as a chariot of liberation, both existentially and eschatologically. My aim is to affirm the Black Church's powerful past and pregnant future and to spark a dialogue that honors our forebears while inspiring this generation to carry the struggle for greater relevance forward.

Contents

Foreword

THE ESSENTIALITY OF THE BLACK CHURCH FOR THE LIFE of the Black community cannot be overstated. One can simply look at Black sociological analyses like that of Du Bois and others who followed in their discipline to see that there is no Black community without the Black church. We do an injustice to any reading of the existence of the Black community without reckoning with this truth. Any scholarship on the nature and character of the Black community, therefore, must always return to discussions of and emphases on the Black Church. Its import, its prominence, and its indispensability can never be forgotten when thinking about the vitality and, indeed, the survival of the community of Black people in the United States of America. It can be stated as a matter of fact that the Black Church is what has kept the Black community alive and enabled it to withstand the onslaught of oppression within the United States.

This is one of the many lessons that the reader will gain from reading Rev. Dr. W. Franklyn Richardson's book. Dr. Richardson is a dear friend of over 40 years. He leads the Conference of National Black Churches, an interdenominational work that helps unite the efforts of Black churches in America. His leadership has allowed him not only to do ministry as a Baptist but also to effect change in other denominational entities. His labor has had ecumenical impact. He is uniquely suited to discuss the importance of the Black Church and how we can push God's agenda forward.

Never Lost: The Black Church as God's Ark of the Covenant argues that the Black Church functions as a divine depository. The culture and communal life are embodied within the Black Church as an institution. What makes the Black community a living community is inextricably bound to the power contained within the Black Church. As a pastor reared by and called to serve within the Black Church, I can readily attest to the unmistakable power of the Black Church to renew and revive a community suffering from derogation. To further elaborate on the chosen image of this book, the Black Church as a holy Ark not only means that it contains the history of the community; it also contains the power that makes its thriving possible.

Rev. Richardson notes, "By linking the Ark of the Covenant to Jesus as Emmanuel, the Black Church becomes a living testament of God's enduring presence and promise. It stands as a place where God's covenant is experienced not only spiritually but also communally—

with us, for us, as us, never having left us, and assuredly coming back for us."

As Dr. Richardson shows us, any reputable reflection on the nature of the Black Church must explore how it had the power to keep the community together. We can look at the Black community at its lowest moment, socially speaking. In the midst of slavery, history tells us we saw an invisible institution arise. Among the enslaved, they found something in common that would bind them together. Their faith in the God who delivered Moses and Daniel made them sing that God would deliver them. Though they were told that being members of the church required listening to Master-approved preachers, they rejected the unwise and oppressive mandates of their oppressors. Slaves would steal away to have "real" church. They would listen to preachers who would not redact the Scripture to teach them false doctrines about their supposed abased status as a people. While they appeared to surrender under the watchful eye of their enslavers, they joined together in submission to a rebellious gospel which taught them of a liberative God. Rules were passed on certain plantations that promised the lash for those who chose to worship independently for no reason. Enslavers knew that the Christianity practiced by the slaves was dangerous for their propagandizing practices. It gave Black people a sense that they were somebody even when they had been stripped of their humanity. It taught them to believe in a God who not only made them in His image and His likeness but sent His Son to die for them and claim them as His people. No matter how virulent racism was for these enslaved people, they came to know that they could be a community because the God of the church had claimed them.

When emancipation occurred, community structure and strength were already available to the formerly enslaved. This sociological phenomenon was only possible because the Black Church had existed. Black people were able to come together as a people because of the integrity afforded by this great institution.

The Black Church has not only functioned this way for the community in the past but ensures a future for the Black community. The 21st century appears to offer nothing but uncertainty and, thereby, insecurity for the Black community. The blowing of the political winds with what seem to be retrograde tendencies within the body politic has caused many to despair of what may become of the Black community. Economically, we are seeing days like those of the Jim Crow era. Educationally, we are seeing little to no progress and decline among Black people. Yet, I can argue that there is hope. Our community's hope rests in the vitality of the Black Church. Since this institution continues to have influence and strength, I can say, without a doubt, our community will not perish. Both our history and our destiny are safe because of God's revelation through the Black Church. Figures like Frederick Douglass, Jarenna Lee, Martin Luther King Jr. and Fannie Lou Hamer will always have heirs. The Black Church will always produce them. The Black Church has been and always will be an institution of liberation through adherence to the gospel of Jesus Christ of Nazareth. We must never forget this and must hold on to this veritable belief.

Dr. Ralph Douglas West
Founder & Senior Pastor
The Church Without Walls, Houston, TX

Preface

FOR CENTURIES, THE BLACK CHURCH HAS BEEN MORE than a place of worship; it is the soul and heartbeat of the Black community. Serving as both a refuge and a source of strength, it has been where faith converges with fortitude and where worship fuels the ongoing pursuit of justice. The Church has provided comfort to the weary, guidance to the lost, and empowerment to the hopeful. From the horrors of slavery to the triumphs of the Civil Rights Movement, and through the trials of the present day, the Black Church has upheld the community like a sacred Ark—safeguarding culture, igniting hope, and fortifying identity against forces that have sought to diminish or erase it.

In many ways, this book is a love letter to that legacy: a legacy of survival, of faith so enduring that it defies the odds, of a people united not just by belief but by shared experience, struggle, and victory. But it is also more than a love letter; it is a summons to action, an urgent call for us to recognize, honor, and renew the Church's place as the cornerstone of our community. This work is both a celebration of what the Black Church has achieved and a vision for what it must continue to be.

We live in times of extraordinary change, facing challenges that are as complex as they are relentless. From systemic racism to economic disparity, from the rise of technology to the pressing need for social justice, our people are met with issues that demand a strong, compassionate, and adaptive Church. The Church must be a place that honors tradition while embracing innovation, a shelter that nurtures the spirit while actively engaging in the fight for equity. This book is a reflection on that calling: a call to see the Black Church not only as a house of worship but as a dynamic, evolving force that addresses the physical, emotional, and spiritual needs of our people.

This work is personal. It is shaped by my own journey in ministry, forged in the fires of hope and heartache, tested and strengthened by the perseverance of those I have served. From my early days as a pastor in Richmond, Virginia and Mount Vernon, New York, to my leadership in the National Baptist Convention and the Conference of National Black Churches and my work in the World Council of Churches, I have witnessed firsthand the power of the Church to transform lives, inspire leaders, and ignite change. I have seen the courage of congregants who find strength in one another, the quiet heroism of lay leaders and choir members who serve with humility, and the power of collective prayer to move mountains.

Through these experiences, I have come to understand that the Church's greatest mission is to serve not just in word but in deed. It is called to be both sanctuary and sword, a place of refuge and a force for justice. The Black Church's role as a dynamic and multidimensional institution is not merely a legacy of its past but a charge for its future. Just as the Ark of the Covenant symbolized God's presence and promises to His people, so too does the Black Church carry forward a sacred mission: to preserve faith, champion justice, and nurture tenacity in the face of adversity.

As I write this book, we have come through some difficult days. Politics, the economy, and the rage of war have gripped all of us with a heavy sense of loss. Over and over, colleagues, parishioners, and friends have called out with repeated questioning: where do we go from here? It is their expression of abandonment and anxiety due to no sense of direction. Their query comes at a time when I have given great thought, while penning this book, to our future direction as African American leaders. It caused me to recollect a time when I rented a car, and the attendant inquired if I would like to access the "Never Lost" electronic guidance system. I replied to the attendant, "What is that?" He explained it was a new guidance system installed in the car, so that wherever you are, you can type in the address and get directions to wherever you desire to go. Inspired by this reflection, the query of these times, and the heavy sense of abandonment and anxiety, the statement of the attendant echoes the question I ask you through these pages, "Do you want 'Never Lost'?"

As you turn these pages, I invite you to join a journey that digs deep into the roots of our history, stands firm in the realities of today, and reaches boldly toward a future still waiting to be built. This book isn't just a story; it's a living tribute to the unshakable faith that has carried the Black community through every challenge and triumph. It's a call to action: to stand together, to lift up the Ark of our shared heritage, and to carry it forward with reverence, strength, and grace.

Let us honor the legacy we have inherited: each hymn sung, each prayer lifted, each act of courage and sacrifice that has woven the rich tapestry of the Black Church. But let us also prepare, steadfastly, for what lies ahead, so that our Church may continue to be a safe haven for all who seek shelter, a place where each soul finds a home and every voice resonates with purpose. May this Church inspire future generations to walk the path of faith, raise their voices for justice, and embody the boundless hope that has always been our greatest inheritance.

This is our legacy, our calling, our sacred mission. May we, the Black Church, take it up with courage and faith, knowing that even when we face loss, we are never truly lost.

Introduction

THE BLACK CHURCH HAS ALWAYS BEEN MORE THAN a building. It has been God's Ark of the Covenant for the Black community. A sacred vessel, it carries our shared culture, values, and faith through the storms of history. Like the Ark in ancient times, it represents God's presence and promise, holding within it not only spiritual truths but also the perseverance, survival, and unyielding hope of a people. Through every challenge and triumph, the Black Church has provided both healing and guidance. It stands as a testament to God's enduring covenant, a living promise that has connected generations through faith.

As we navigate a rapidly changing world, the Black Church's role as this Ark has never been more vital. The challenges we face may look different today—shaped by technology, global connectivity, and shifting social landscapes—but the Church's mission endures. This book is both a tribute to its transformative history and a rallying cry for its ongoing relevance. The Church is not simply a place of worship; it is a beacon of hope for generations, offering strength, empowerment, and unity to move forward with purpose.

Now more than ever, we must cherish and preserve the Church's role as the keeper of our history, values, and aspirations. It is through this sacred mission that we find purpose and the promise of a future rooted in justice, faith, and community. The Black Church must remain the foundation for empowerment and endurance, carrying forward its legacy as a guide in an uncertain world.

The Heartbeat of Our Community

Throughout history, the Black Church has been the heartbeat of African American identity. In times of darkness, it was a refuge; in moments of triumph, it was a celebration. During the era of slavery, it provided solace and spiritual resistance. Through the civil rights movement, it became a wellspring of courage and strategy, standing as a center of community empowerment. Today, it offers clarity and unity in the fight against systemic injustice. But the Church's role extends beyond preserving traditions. It has continuously adapted, blending cultural pride with faith to serve as a wellspring of hope for generations.

Within its sacred walls, stories are told, legacies are honored, and values are passed from one generation to the next. As Black communities face new challenges—

from economic struggles and mental health crises to systemic inequities and cultural threats—the Church's role as a stabilizing and unifying force is more critical than ever. It is the foundation upon which the community's strength and spirit are built.

A Call to Action for the Black Church

We live in an era defined by remarkable technological advancements and global connectivity, yet paradoxically, many feel more isolated and marginalized than ever before. In this landscape, the Black Church must not only adapt but lead with purpose. Historically, the Church has served as both sanctuary and sword, addressing the spiritual and social needs of its community. This dual role remains as crucial today as ever.

The Black Church must renew its commitment to preserving the cultural identity and spiritual backbone of Black communities. It has served as a stabilizing force, fostering unity and empowerment through collective action and faith.

This book calls on leaders, congregants, and scholars to embrace the Church's sacred mission of safeguarding history while envisioning a bold future. The Black Church bears witness to faith, fortitude, and justice across generations. This Ark of our collective heritage must continue to inspire and guide the community forward, ensuring that the legacy of Black culture and spirituality remains vibrant, respected, and transformative.

My Journey in Ministry

This call to action is deeply personal, grounded in my six decades of ministry. My pastoral journey began in Richmond, Virginia, where I was moved by the tenacity of people facing significant economic hardship who remained steadfast in their faith. Later, in Mount Vernon, New York, I encountered the complexities of urban ministry, working in a diverse environment filled with unique challenges and opportunities for leadership. These experiences taught me that the Black Church must remain flexible and responsive, able to meet the people where they are while never wavering in its foundational principles.

In my role as General Secretary of the National Baptist Convention, I saw the power of unity among Black Churches nationwide, advancing a shared mission of faith and justice. This unity was further amplified in my work as Chair of the Conference of National Black Churches, where I engaged with faith leaders from across the country and witnessed firsthand how our combined efforts could create change. These experiences reinforced my belief that the strength of the Black Church lies in our unity and shared commitment to justice and equality.

The Global and Ecumenical Legacy

My ministry has also taken me beyond American borders, offering a global perspective on the Black Church's role as a bastion of hope and cultural preservation. From rural churches in the American South to townships in South Africa, I have seen the profound impact of the Black Church on the lives of Black people around the world. This legacy transcends boundaries, bearing witness to the endurance, creativity, and unyielding pursuit of justice that defines the Black Church. It serves as a cultural and spiritual refuge for those in need, a wellspring of hope for those facing oppression, and a powerful force for change that resonates across continents.

The Path Forward

The chapters ahead explore in detail the many dimensions of the Black Church: its role as a hub of community life, a protector of cultural heritage, and a relentless advocate for justice. They examine the Church's prophetic voice, which has boldly called for justice and challenged oppression throughout history. These chapters also look to the future, emphasizing the critical need for intergenerational leadership, technological adaptability, and mentorship to ensure the Black Church remains an impactful and vibrant institution in the years to come.

Before we proceed, it is crucial to clarify a common misunderstanding. Many people conflate the physical gathering of Black individuals in a church setting with the spiritual entity of the Black Church. However, the Black Church, as envisioned in this work, is not merely a building or a gathering. It is a sacred community of faith, bound by a shared commitment to worship, fellowship, and the presence of God. Much like the Ark of the Covenant, the Black Church represents a spiritual covenant between God and His people. Preserving this understanding is essential to honoring the authenticity and legacy of the Black Church.

Preserving and Building for the Future

The Black Church has always been a steady anchor for Black communities, but its job isn't just to protect the past. It's about creating a future where the next generation can inherit a Church that stays connected to its roots while addressing today's challenges. The Church has been a center of empowerment and perseverance, creating spaces for community and leadership even in the face of systemic challenges. This enduring role inspires current and future leaders to carry the Ark of the Covenant with respect, courage, and a deep commitment to service.

As the Black Church explores new ways to reach people, like using technology and fresh approaches to ministry, it must stay rooted in the timeless principles of its faith. By balancing innovation with tradition, the Church can remain a vibrant force for the future.

Honoring Legacy

This book honors the lasting legacy of the Black Church while presenting a vision for its continued relevance and impact. The Black Church has always been more than a place of worship; it has been a school, a meeting hall, and a social service center. During slavery, the Black Church served as both a refuge and a foundation for resistance. It has also been a community hub, fostering leadership and cultural pride.

Through slavery, segregation, and systemic exclusion, the Black Church has been a vessel for carrying Black communities forward, embodying resilience, identity, and hope. As we move into the future, we are called to uphold and expand this legacy, ensuring the Black Church remains the Ark of the Covenant for Black people: a guiding light and unshakable foundation for generations to come.

A Call to Leaders, Scholars, and Congregants

To all who serve in the Black Church—from preachers in the pulpit to lay leaders, choir members, and faithful congregants—this is your call to action. The Black Church has always thrived on the collective effort of its people, each person playing a role in building a community grounded in faith.

Leaders, this is the time to foster intergenerational collaboration, mentoring the next generation to carry the torch with courage and creativity. Scholars, your research and teaching illuminate the Church's past and guide its future. Congregants, your steadfast faith and participation sustain the Church's heartbeat. Together, we all contribute to preserving the Black Church as a sacred vessel: a living Ark that carries the hopes, struggles, and triumphs of its people forward.

This work is a reminder of who we are and what we can achieve when united in purpose. Let us engage deeply with the sacred task of carrying the Ark, ensuring that the Black Church continues to inspire, uplift, and transform lives for the times ahead.

NEVER
LOST

1

The Black Church
as God's Ark
of the Covenant

In the stillness of a desert morning, the Ark of the Covenant glimmered faintly, its golden surface catching the first rays of sunlight. This was no ordinary artifact; it was a sacred vessel, crafted with divine instruction to symbolize the covenant between God and His people. Within its consecrated interior lay the stone tablets of the Law, Aaron's budding staff, and a jar of manna, each representing God's guidance, provision, and promise. Carried by the Levites through wilderness and war, the Ark was more than a relic; it was a living testament to God's unbroken presence and His covenant with Israel.

Similarly, the Black Church has been a sacred vessel, bearing the collective faith, perseverance, and hopes of Black communities through the trials of history. Like the Ark, the Church has carried the weight of divine promises, navigating the turbulent waters of slavery, segregation, and systemic oppression. It has been a shelter for the weary, a place where faith meets action, and where God's covenant of justice and liberation is reaffirmed.

The Church holds the stories of its people, the hymns of hope, the prayers whispered in despair, and the cries for justice. It moves forward, not on the shoulders of priests but through the strength of a united community, bound by faith and an unyielding belief in God's promises. This chapter explores the Black Church's role as a modern Ark of the Covenant, reflecting on its historical significance, cultural impact, and spiritual mission.

The Black Church's Role in Black Life

The Black Church has always been more than a place of worship; it serves as a sanctuary, a rallying point, and a cornerstone of cultural identity. W.E.B. Du Bois called the Black Church "the social centre of Negro life in the United States" and a critical "refuge in a hostile world" (as cited in Barber 2015, p. 246), describing its importance in providing essential resources and opportunities for Black communities amid racial inequalities. Barber argues that the Black Church has historically occupied a complex role, simultaneously accommodating and resisting societal norms depending on the context, thus making it an essential institution capable of addressing social issues where governmental support has diminished. From its origins as an "invisible institution" during slavery to its modern incarnation, the Church has consistently expanded its impact beyond spiritual guidance, influencing education, political activism, community development, and cultural preservation (Barber, 2015).

Historical Significance and Social Impact

To understand the Black Church's evolution, we must travel back to its origins within the "invisible institution" that operated under the conditions of slavery. These early gatherings were, by necessity, conducted in secrecy, hidden from watchful eyes that sought to control the bodies and spirits of enslaved people (Allen, 2023). Here, in the covert spaces of worship, enslaved Black people forged a spiritual resistance, developing a theology that affirmed their dignity and humanity. The "invisible institution" became the foundation of the Black Church, a place where hope was nurtured and identity was preserved amidst dehumanizing conditions.

The Black Church's impact extended beyond religion to encompass social and political dimensions, particularly during the Civil Rights Movement, when churches became organizing centers, safe havens, and platforms for activism. Rev. Ralph David Abernathy used the Church's teachings to inspire a generation. As a co-founder of the Southern Christian Leadership Conference (SCLC) and leader in the Montgomery Bus Boycott, his faith and dedication highlighted the Black Church's role in social change. The Church's ability to serve as both a priestly and a prophetic institution reflected its unique capacity to blend worship with a call for societal change, supporting the community through both spiritual nourishment and active resistance.

Providing Moral and Spiritual Guidance in Social Contexts

Throughout history, the Black Church has turned to the Bible to address real-life challenges. Through uplifting sermons, justice-focused teachings, and practical community programs, it connects faith with people's everyday realities.

Black preachers are at the heart of this work, showing the courage and wisdom needed to help heal the wounds caused by centuries of oppression. In many ways, they carry on a sacred tradition, offering both spiritual guidance and a strong moral voice.

Rev. Al Sharpton speaks powerfully about how Black communities still suffer from the physical, emotional, and mental trauma caused by enslaving people and treating them as less than cattle (Sharpton & Hunger, 2002). In response, Black preachers take on two important tasks: offering spiritual support and speaking out against the lasting pain created by historic injustices. By blending faith with an honest look at the past, they protect both the memory and the dignity of their people.

Rev. Sharpton also brings up the topic of reparations, describing it as debt that is owed to people for crimes that were committed against their ancestors (Sharpton & Hunger, 2002). In many Black churches, preachers are the ones who raise these issues, pointing to the Ark of the Covenant as a symbol of God's justice and commitment to the oppressed. In the same way, they affirm the worth of those who have been mistreated, striving for healing on both spiritual and societal levels.

In this spirit, Black preachers guide the Church to be both a haven and a rallying point: a place that comforts people and pushes them to take action. Historian and Civil Rights advocate Gayraud S. Wilmore (1998) describes this role, noting how the Black Church has served as both a refuge that provides solace and a rallying point to demand action. Through passionate preaching, believers gain hope and resolve to face ongoing injustices, relying on the powerful memory of God's faithfulness. Here again, the Black Church becomes like a modern Ark of the Covenant, where divine promises spur people on to seek justice.

By combining faith leadership with a push for social change, Black preachers ensure the Church remains a strong source of empowerment. Much like the Israelites carrying the Ark, the Black community carries forward a story of steadfast faith and the drive to overcome oppression. Along the way, the Church stands as a living sign of God's presence—Emmanuel—lifting its people and urging them toward freedom and wholeness.

Origins and Purpose of the Black Church

The purpose of the Black Church emerged out of necessity. As Allen (2023) notes, "the Black Church, from its outset as the 'invisible institution' within slavery, has always served the Black community ... " (p. 2). It was established as a space for worship free from the exclusionary practices of White Christians, who often denied Black people a place within their congregations. In separating from White churches, Black Christians found the freedom to express a spirituality that resonated with their experiences, needs, and heritage. The Black Church thus became not only a spiritual refuge but also a community institution where Black identity was affirmed and celebrated.

Much like the Ark of the Covenant symbolized God's promises to Israel, the Black Church embodies a covenant of liberation, justice, and hope for its community. It is an institution where faith fortifies resilience and worship binds individuals in a shared identity. Here, God's promises are renewed, offering strength to confront the ongoing challenges of Black life in America.

The Ark of the Covenant: A Biblical Foundation

As previously mentioned, the Ark of the Covenant was a sacred vessel that embodied God's steadfast covenant with Israel. Crafted according to divine instructions (*New King James Version*, 1982, Exodus 25:10–22), the Ark contained three sacred items: the tablets of the Law, Aaron's rod, and a jar of manna. Each of these objects symbolized a vital aspect of God's relationship with His people—His authority, provision, and guidance—standing as tangible reminders of His promises and presence.

Housed within the Holy of Holies in the tabernacle, the Ark represented not only God's holiness but also His intimate involvement in the lives of His people. It was a visible reminder of God's commitment to journey with them through every trial and triumph. Each movement of the Ark reaffirmed that God was neither distant nor indifferent; He was actively present, guiding His people with faithfulness and purpose toward a future filled with hope.

Symbolism and Sacred Artifacts in the Ark

The Ark of the Covenant held profound symbolic meaning, reflecting the depth of God's relationship with Israel. Each sacred item within the Ark represented a fundamental aspect of faith, provision, and divine guidance. Together, they formed a covenant built on trust, law, and sustenance: qualities that resonate with the Black Church's mission as a modern Ark of God's promises.

The Tablets of the Law

At the core of the Ark were the Tablets of the Law, divinely inscribed commandments given to Moses on Mount Sinai. These tablets were more than guidelines; they were a covenant: a binding agreement between Yahweh and His people, deeply tied to Israel's prophetic and moral traditions. Rather than serving as a restrictive burden, these laws provided a moral foundation that guided Israel in righteousness and communal harmony. In this manner, the commandments, as fulfilled joyfully through Christ, transform duty into delight.

The Black Church mirrors this covenant in its steadfast commitment to biblical principles and its dedication to justice, mercy, and love. Like the tablets that reminded Israel of its divine obligations, the Black Church upholds ethical standards, acting as a moral guide during times of injustice and adversity. Its teachings inspire perseverance and foster social renewal, providing a blueprint for hope and a pathway to a compassionate, just society.

Aaron's Rod as a Symbol of Leadership

Aaron's rod, housed within the Ark, symbolizes God's anointing of chosen leaders. This staff, which miraculously budded, signified divine authority and served as evidence of God's power to appoint leaders to shepherd His people. The rod, once a simple tool, became a sacred emblem of God's active involvement in guiding His community.

Similarly, the Black Church has long embodied this role of leadership, raising up clergy and activists to guide communities through faith and social transformation. Figures like Reverend Al Sharpton, whose National Action Network continues to advance the cause of social justice, Reverend Dr. William J. Barber II, with his modern Poor People's Campaign, and Reverend Raphael Warnock, pastor of Ebenezer Baptist Church and U.S. Senator, continue this legacy. Their leadership reflects the Black Church's enduring mission to inspire justice and equality while serving as a moral compass. As I have written in *Speaking Truth to Power: The Role of the Black Church in Social Justice* (Richardson, 2020), "The Church must be the vessel that carries God's promises through the storm, just as the Ark carried the promise through the wilderness."

The rod's symbolism is further enriched by its connection to spiritual transformation. Preacher and author Charles Spurgeon (1863; 1895) notes that spiritual consciousness can bring about material change, echoing the Black Church's role in cultivating leaders who inspire progress. Historical figures like Fannie Lou Hamer and

Dr. Martin Luther King Jr. epitomize this sacred calling, wielding the authority of Aaron's rod to lead with faith and courage. Their legacy continues to affirm the Church's role as both guide and protector, carrying forward God's promise of leadership through transformative action.

The Jar of Manna as Provision

The jar of manna within the Ark served as a reminder of God's provision during Israel's wilderness journey. This "bread from heaven" symbolized God's continual sustenance, offering daily nourishment in barren lands. Spurgeon (1889; 1895) highlights manna as a testament to God's faithful care, both physical and spiritual, emphasizing His willingness to meet the deepest needs of His people. It represented not only sustenance but also a divine assurance that His care would remain constant, even in times of desolation.

The Black Church has long embraced this role of provision, acting as both spiritual sustainer and community support system. During slavery, through the Civil Rights Movement, and into the present, the Church has provided its members with essential resources, ranging from food and shelter to hope and spiritual fortitude. Just as manna descended to nourish the Israelites daily, the Black Church has served as a steady source of staying power, encouraging its community to persevere and trust in God's abundant provision.

Spurgeon (1970) observed, "In the wilderness there fell more manna than the tribes could eat and more water than the hosts could drink," reminding us that divine provision often exceeds human need. In the same way, the Black Church has nurtured its members through prayer, worship, and collective support, reinforcing the belief that God's care knows no bounds. By fostering faith in God's sufficiency, the Church transforms challenges into opportunities for growth and robustness.

The jar of manna also symbolizes communal strength and hope, affirming that God's provision extends to every area of life. The Black Church, through its ministries and outreach, embodies this assurance, offering not only material aid but also the spiritual sustenance necessary to face life's struggles. It reminds its community that God's care is both vast and intimate, ensuring that no one journeys alone. The Church, like the manna, continues to nourish, sustain, and inspire, reinforcing the enduring promise of God's presence and provision.

Theological Significance of the Ark in Israelite Tradition

The Ark of the Covenant symbolized God's unshakable bond with Israel—a covenant built on trust, law, and sustenance—qualities that resonate with the Black Church's mission as a modern Ark of God's promises.

Covenant and Divine Presence

Spurgeon (1895) wrote, "In that Ark ... we would have seen, first, God dwelling among men. What a wonderful thing!" (p. 5). The Ark wasn't just a container; it was proof that God was with His people, walking alongside them through every challenge. For the Israelites, the Ark was a constant reassurance that God wasn't watching from a distance; He was present, guiding and protecting them.

In much the same way, the Black Church stands as a vessel of God's presence. It has been a place where faith meets action and where God's closeness is felt during life's hardest moments. Like the Ark, the Church offers a space where individuals can find strength, hope, and the courage to face both personal struggles and societal injustices, knowing that God is in it with them.

Moral Obligations and Community Duty

The Ark also came with responsibilities. It reminded the Israelites of their covenant with God and with each other. It wasn't just about rules; it was a call to live with integrity, justice, and faithfulness.

The Black Church carries forward this same legacy of moral accountability. It doesn't just teach about faith: it calls its members to act, to stand for justice, and to build strong communities. It's a place where worship inspires action, reminding everyone of their shared duty to uphold God's vision of equality and love.

This is where the Black Church shines—not just as a refuge but as a guide. It challenges individuals to live out their faith in ways that transform lives and communities. Like the Ark of old, the Church carries forward God's promises, lighting the way through the challenges of today's world and calling everyone to stay true to God's covenant.

The Black Church as a Sacred Vessel

Like the Ark, the Black Church has long been a symbol of hope. More than a place of worship, it has embodied strength and divine assurance through the darkest periods of history. From the brutal realities of slavery to the oppressive structures of Jim Crow and systemic discrimination, the Church has affirmed the enduring presence of God, offering a spiritual foundation that transcends suffering and fuels the belief in liberation and justice.

Emerging in secrecy during slavery, the Black Church was a place where enslaved individuals could gather away from the watchful eyes of their oppressors. These covert gatherings provided space for worship, collective struggle, and the cultivation of a theology rooted in hope and deliverance. Within these hidden spaces, resilience was nurtured through whispered prayers, hymns, and sermons that echoed a profound belief in God's power to liberate.

This theology of liberation became central to the Church's mission and transformed it into a force for spiritual and communal empowerment (Cone, 1997). It continues to serve as a vessel of God's promises, carrying forward the conviction that God walks alongside the downtrodden and offering strength and hope to persevere against oppression.

The Black Church as a Spiritual Refuge

The Black Church has long been a place of safety and fortitude within the Black community. Barnes (2023) describes the Church as a bulwark, a safe space where individuals and families facing a hostile society could find collective strength. Here, individuals could cast off the burdens of oppression, if only temporarily, and immerse themselves in an environment of mutual care, support, and spiritual healing. Unlike any other institution, the Black Church offered a unique blend of spiritual shelter and social refuge, allowing Black people to feel embraced by both God and community.

The Church's significance extended beyond the individual. It was—and is—a place of shared stories and collective memory. Each Sunday, the community gathers not just for worship but for affirmation of their identity and value. In this sacred space, each voice, each hymn, and each prayer reverberates with the power of ancestral fortitude. The Church has become a place where individuals could affirm their humanity and receive dignity often denied elsewhere.

Ark of Empowerment:
The Black Church as Sacred Pillars

The Black Church has always been more than a Sunday morning gathering. It's a cornerstone of identity and community for African Americans. In many ways, it serves a role similar to the Ark of the Covenant for the Israelites, standing as a symbol of sanctity and strength in the face of challenges. Both are sacred pillars, reminding their people of who they are, where they've been, and the divine presence that walks with them every step of the way.

Symbolic Architecture and Divine Presence

Just as the Black Church is no ordinary gathering, the Ark of the Covenant wasn't just a box covered in gold. It was a reminder that God was close by, traveling alongside the Israelites no matter where life took them (May, 1936). In much the same way, the Black Church is more than just a building. It's a place where people come to feel God's presence, find comfort, and recharge their spirits.

Whether it's the powerful lift of a gospel choir or the quiet reassurance of a prayer circle, the Church offers a sense of belonging and peace. Its familiar hymns, welcoming spaces, and community gatherings remind everyone who walks through its doors that they're not alone. Just as the Ark reminded the Israelites that God was with them on their journey, the Black Church stands as a symbol of hope and a reminder that God is always near, even in life's toughest moments.

Tradition and Cultural Identity

For the Israelites, the Ark of the Covenant stood at the heart of their faith and culture, a touchstone that guided them through their trials and triumphs (May, 1936). In a similar vein, the Black Church has been a cornerstone of African American identity, preserving and celebrating the deep connection between spiritual practices and cultural heritage.

The Church serves as a living archive of Black traditions, where songs carry the weight of history, sermons give voice to endurance, and rituals strengthen the ties of community. It's a place where pride and purpose are nurtured, and where values are passed down like heirlooms. Just as the Ark grounded the Israelites in their sense of self, the Black Church continues to fortify its community, reminding them of their collective strength and the firm foundation on which they stand.

Liberation as a Covenant Promise

At its heart, the promise of liberation carried by the Ark of the Covenant was a divine assurance: a commitment to free the oppressed and uplift the downtrodden. The Black Church carries this legacy forward, living out God's promise of freedom in both spiritual and practical ways. Throughout history, it has been a guiding light, a source of strength, and a rallying point for those seeking justice. In the same way that the Ark represented deliverance for the Israelites, the Black Church has offered pathways to liberation for its community, weaving God's call for justice into every prayer, sermon, and hymn.

This is more than history; it's a living tradition. For generations, the Black Church has stood as a voice for the marginalized, declaring that God is not distant but deeply present in the struggles of the oppressed. Whether in the hushed secrecy of hidden worship during slavery, the galvanizing sermons of civil rights leaders, or the ongoing fight for equity and social justice, the Church has always been both a safe haven and a launchpad for change.

It's a sacred space where theology meets lived experience—a place where faith becomes action. From its pulpits and pews rise calls for justice that are not just words but catalysts for transformation. The gospel of Jesus is a gospel of liberation that calls for a radical transformation of people as individuals and as a community (Cone, 1997). The Black Church affirms that God's justice is active and urgent, a force that uplifts the brokenhearted and fuels the fight for liberation. In doing so, it reminds us all that the promise of freedom is not confined to scripture but lives on in every act of perseverance and hope.

A Theology of Hope and Action

The theology of liberation at the heart of the Black Church is fundamentally a theology of hope. It asserts that oppression does not have the final word and that God's justice will ultimately prevail. This belief fuels the Church's mission, pushing it beyond the confines of its walls to engage actively with the broader society.

The Black Church pairs faith with tangible action through initiatives like voter mobilization, economic empowerment programs, and community outreach. These efforts exemplify how spirituality and activism can combine to bring about lasting change. The Church's prophetic voice holds systems and individuals accountable while simultaneously encouraging communities to envision and work toward a world marked by greater equity and justice. Through its theology of hope and action, the Black Church continues to inspire faith that is both transformational and rooted in love.

Liberation Theology in the Black Church

The concept of liberation theology is deeply interwoven with the identity and mission of the Black Church, reflecting the belief that faith must move beyond personal salvation to engage with social justice. This theology asserts that the gospel is not only a message of individual redemption but also a call to collective liberation. Dr. James H. Cone (1997) described liberation theology as the gospel for Black Churches. Liberation theology emphasizes Jesus as a liberator who stands with the oppressed, actively working to dismantle systems of injustice and restore the dignity of those marginalized by society.

Historical Foundation of Liberation Theology

The origins of liberation theology in the Black Church are grounded in the experiences of enslaved African Americans, who crafted a theology of resilience and liberation amidst their suffering. These hidden congregations became spiritual havens where the enslaved could reimagine the Christian narrative as one of empowerment. The story of the Exodus, with its themes of deliverance from bondage, became a cornerstone of Black spirituality. Through prayers, songs, and sermons, these gatherings forged a theological framework that affirmed freedom as both a divine promise and a moral imperative.

Cornel West, in *Prophesy Deliverance!* (1982), highlights how this reinterpretation of Christian theology blended spirituality with revolutionary consciousness, fostering a tradition of resistance that continues to shape the Black

Church's identity. These sacred spaces were not only spiritual sanctuaries but also incubators of hope and activism, laying the groundwork for the Church's role in movements for social justice, from abolition to civil rights.

The Church as an Advocate for the Oppressed

Advocating for the oppressed has never been an optional calling for the Black Church; it is central to its identity as a sacred institution. The Black Church has embodied liberation theology (Cone, 1997). This role demands a mission that extends beyond worship, encompassing social justice and the empowerment of marginalized communities. The Church has long amplified the voices of the silenced, serving as a prophetic witness against societal norms and systems that sustain inequality.

For generations, the Black Church has been a moral compass, boldly confronting injustice and standing in solidarity with the marginalized. Its legacy of advocacy is evident in its pivotal role during the Civil Rights Movement and remains vital today as it addresses modern struggles like police brutality, economic inequality, and disparities in education. Within its walls, the Church reinforces the inherent worth and dignity of every individual, reminding its community of their divine right to freedom, even when society attempts to deny them these fundamental truths.

The Black Church does more than provide comfort. It shines the light of divine presence, guiding its people through the deserts of discrimination and the valleys of despair. Its mission is not merely to bear witness but to inspire action, empowering its congregation to face oppression with fortitude and hope, firmly grounded in faith and justice.

The Black Church's Activism Legacy

The Black Church has always been a wellspring of action and change. During the Civil Rights Movement, churches became the nerve centers of strategy and organization, hosting meetings, voter registration drives, and nonviolent protests. Church leaders took on dual roles, serving not only as spiritual guides but also as community strategists and activists, rallying their congregations toward meaningful social transformation. These sacred spaces became both sanctuaries of hope and arenas of action, where the promise of liberation was translated into concrete steps toward equality.

Far from being passive observers, the Church and its leaders carried forward the covenant of justice, embodying the belief that faith must be lived out through action. Religious scholar Albert J. Raboteau (2004) describes the Church's role in fostering resistance and resilience as rooted in a deep tradition of faith-driven advocacy. These moments in history reinforce the enduring truth that liberation is not merely a promise to be spoken about but a mission to be enacted. The legacy of activism within the Black Church serves as both an inspiration and a challenge, reminding us that the fight for justice continues, and our faith calls us to confront injustice wherever it persists.

Today, the National Action Network (NAN), founded by Rev. Sharpton in 1991, continues this legacy, serving as a critical platform for clergy and congregations committed to civil rights advocacy and social justice. With chapters nationwide, NAN mobilizes communities, uniting faith with political and economic empowerment, thus keeping alive the Black Church's longstanding tradition of activism and leadership (https://nationalactionnetwork.net).

Modern Social Justice Movements

The Black Church continues to stand as a prophetic voice, calling society to account and urging justice and equality. Whether addressing systemic racism, economic inequities, or disparities in education, the Church remains a guiding light for its community, consistently reminding us that God's promises are not confined to history; they are alive, relevant, and still unfolding. By engaging in movements like Black Lives Matter and other justice initiatives, the Black Church demonstrates its commitment to carrying forward the covenant of liberation, building on its historical role as both spiritual refuge and agent of change.

This mission is as vital now as it ever was. The Black Church reminds its members—and society at large—that God's promise of freedom isn't something we merely read about in scripture. It's an active call to rise against injustice, to defend human dignity, and to ensure that equity becomes a lived reality. Within the Church's sacred walls, faith becomes action, offering the moral courage to challenge oppression and work toward a future that reflects the justice, compassion, and hope that define God's covenant. Rev. Sharpton emphasizes that the Church must remain steadfast, continually working to rebuild society's moral foundations through active faith-rooted advocacy and justice-driven activism (Sharpton & Hunger, 2002).

Preservation of Sacred Traditions

The Black Church stands as a vital keeper of sacred traditions, nurturing spiritual and cultural identity while providing continuity across generations. These traditions, much like the Ark of the Covenant for the Israelites, serve as tangible reminders of faith and perseverance. Just as the Ark carried the tablets of the Law, Aaron's rod, and manna as symbols of divine guidance and provision, the Black Church embodies its own legacy of resilience and hope through practices that sustain and empower its community (Raboteau, 2004).

Elements like gospel music, spirituals, and call-and-response preaching are deeply embedded in the Church's DNA. These are not simply forms of expression; they are acts of spiritual affirmation, passed down as a living testament to God's presence and faithfulness. Each hymn, prayer, and sermon resonates with the shared history of struggle and triumph, binding past and present in a unified voice of faith.

We will discuss the preservation of such traditions in detail in coming chapters.

The Black Church in the Wilderness of Modernity

The journey of the Israelites through the wilderness, with the Ark of the Covenant at their center, was one of profound challenges: grappling with survival, identity, and faith in the face of uncertainty. Similarly, the Black Church now finds itself navigating its own wilderness in the modern era. The 21st century has ushered in rapid cultural shifts, evolving values, and new societal pressures. Declining membership, generational divides, and the rise of secularism all pose significant challenges, threatening the Church's longstanding influence and its role as a pillar of the community (Glaude, 2020).

In this contemporary wilderness, the Black Church must adapt to meet the needs of emerging generations while remaining steadfast in its sacred mission. The Church's role as a beacon of hope and a vessel of God's covenant has not diminished, but the strategies it employs must evolve. New models of engagement—embracing digital ministry, fostering intergenerational dialogue, and addressing pressing social issues—are vital for the Church to continue carrying forward God's promises.

Just as the Israelites found strength in the Ark as a guiding symbol of divine presence, the Black Church must reaffirm its covenantal role by embodying fortitude, unity, and faith. This is a time to draw from its rich history of overcoming adversity and to apply those lessons in fresh, innovative ways. By balancing its enduring values with new approaches, the Church can continue to serve as a spiritual and cultural anchor for the community, offering guidance and hope in the ever-changing landscape of modernity.

Generational and Ideological Challenges

Generational Divide in Religious Practices

One of the most significant challenges confronting the Black Church today is the widening generational divide in religious practices and values. Younger generations, shaped by a rapidly changing world, often approach the Church with skepticism or disengagement, viewing it as disconnected from their realities. While older congregants may find solace in traditional services and rituals, younger individuals often seek an experience that is culturally relevant, inclusive, and responsive to contemporary issues such as social justice, climate change, and mental health.

The rise of the "nones"—those who identify as having no particular religious affiliation—has further complicated this divide. This trend, particularly pronounced among younger demographics, signals a growing disconnection from institutional religion. Many in this group feel that the Church does not adequately address their concerns or reflect their lived experiences, leading them to search for meaning outside the bounds of formal religious spaces or to reject organized religion altogether.

This generational divide presents the Black Church with a critical challenge: how can it remain faithful to its core values and traditions while evolving to meet the spiritual and social needs of younger generations? To bridge this gap, the Church must cultivate spaces for honest dialogue between generations, embracing change where necessary without losing sight of its covenantal mission. By addressing pressing issues relevant to younger congregants, incorporating diverse perspectives into its leadership, and adapting its methods of outreach, the Black Church can reaffirm its role as a spiritual and cultural cornerstone for all generations.

Secularism and Evolving Belief Systems

The Black Church faces a new challenge: keeping its message relevant in a world where spirituality often steps outside traditional religious boundaries. A secular exploration of spirituality has presented unique challenges for the Black Church. Many people, especially those of younger generations, are exploring spirituality on their own terms in ways that are often untethered from organized religion. From personal spirituality to skepticism about institutions, today's religious landscape is shifting, and the Church is grappling with how to maintain its central role in this evolving narrative.

For many, this shift reflects a craving for authenticity, transparency, and justice: qualities deeply rooted in the Black Church's mission but sometimes viewed as absent in practice. As more people embrace a spiritual life outside formal structures, they're still searching for meaning, connection, and a sense of purpose. This presents a challenge but also a chance for the Church to reimagine its message and outreach.

The path forward might involve bridging tradition with innovation: meeting people where they are while staying true to the Church's values of community and liberation. Whether it's through tackling real-world issues head-on or creating spaces for open dialogue and creativity, the Black Church has an opportunity to show that it can remain a vital source of hope and belonging in a rapidly changing world. It's about adjusting to the times without losing what makes the Church a stronghold of faith and perseverance.

Embracing the Modern Wilderness as an Opportunity

The modern wilderness, though fraught with challenges, offers the Black Church an extraordinary opportunity to reimagine itself while remaining steadfast in its sacred mission. Just as the Israelites discovered strength and purpose during their wilderness journey, the Church can find renewal and vision in this period of transformation. The wilderness is not only a place of testing; it is a place of revelation, where new possibilities emerge and foundational truths are reaffirmed.

Seeing Challenges as Pathways to Renewal

Rather than viewing the obstacles of declining membership, generational divides, and secular shifts as insurmountable, the Church can approach them as pathways to a renewed sense of purpose. Each challenge carries within it the potential for growth and deeper connection. The wilderness, in this context, becomes a space for boldness, creativity, and spiritual awakening. It calls for a fresh look at how the Church can minister to a community navigating the complexities of modern life.

Bold Adaptations for a Prophetic Mission

This moment invites the Church to embrace new tools and perspectives that allow it to meet people where they are. By leveraging technology, engaging more actively in social justice initiatives, and creating inclusive spaces that welcome diverse voices, the Church can reinforce its role as a prophetic voice and a refuge for those seeking hope and belonging. The Church needs boldness, courage and adaptability in times of change, qualities that will be crucial as it navigates this wilderness moment.

Anchored in Principles, Open to Possibility

What makes this opportunity so unique is the potential to blend innovation with enduring principles. The Church can adapt without abandoning the values that have defined it for generations. By holding fast to its commitment to justice, love, and community, the Black Church can ensure that its mission remains relevant and impactful, even in an ever-changing world.

In embracing the modern wilderness, the Black Church reaffirms its identity as a guiding light for the community. It transforms challenges into opportunities, ensuring that it continues to serve as a source of strength and a force for positive change for generations to come.

The Enduring Mission of the Black Church

The Black Church's ability to adapt while preserving its core mission has been its defining strength through centuries of struggle and triumph. Much like the Ark of the Covenant carried by the Israelites, the Church continues to bear God's promises, serving as a testament to His enduring presence and faithfulness. In the face of modern challenges, the Church must remain steadfast: a sacred vessel of love and justice, bringing light to dark places and hope to uncertain times.

This journey through modernity calls on the Black Church to balance tradition and transformation. By staying rooted in its principles of faith and justice while embracing change, the Church ensures its continued relevance and vitality, offering guidance and strength to its community in an ever-evolving world.

2

Emmanuel, God With Us: The Black Church and a New Testament Hope

REFLECTING ON THE THEMES OF "EMMANUEL: GOD WITH US" (Richardson, 2006a), I am reminded of the enduring witness of God's presence throughout Scripture. In the Old Testament, the Ark of the Covenant functioned as far more than a sacred object; it was a powerful emblem of God's commitment to dwell among His people. As mentioned in the last chapter, the Ark was crafted according to divine instruction and contained the tablets of the Law, Aaron's staff, and a jar of manna: each representing God's guidance, provision, and steadfast love toward the Israelites (*New King James Version*, 1982, Exodus 25:10–22). These items anchored the community in God's abiding presence, giving them confidence and hope during their wilderness journey.

In the New Testament, this covenantal promise reaches a deeper level through the Incarnation of Jesus Christ, identified as Emmanuel—"God with us" (*New King*

James Version, 1982, Matthew 1:23). Where the Ark once embodied the reality of divine presence through sacred symbols, Jesus fulfills and surpasses those symbols by arriving in human form. In Christ, God's faithfulness is no longer contained within a holy vessel but is revealed through a living, personal relationship with humanity. He becomes the ultimate expression of God's nearness and love, drawing people into communion with the divine in ways the Ark only foreshadowed.

The transition from the Ark to Christ signals a remarkable shift in how God's covenant is experienced. Once represented by a sacred chest housing tokens of God's promise, Emmanuel now embodies that promise in a dynamic, intimate way, walking with God's people through every trial and triumph. This truth resonates profoundly within the Black Church, which has long cherished and proclaimed God's liberating presence in its historical struggles and victories. At its core, Emmanuel invites us to recognize a God who is not confined to relics of the past but is alive among us, actively sharing in the everyday realities of His people.

Significance of "Emmanuel" in Christian Theology

Definition and Biblical Origin of "Emmanuel"

The name "Emmanuel" emerges in the prophetic text of Isaiah 7:14 (*New King James Version*, 1982), which proclaims that a virgin will bear a son named Emmanuel, revealing God's direct involvement with His people. In the New Testament, this prophecy finds its fulfillment in the birth of Jesus, whose very life demonstrates God's desire to be among humanity—not as an aloof deity but as a compassionate companion walking alongside people through every season (*New King James Version*, 1982, Matthew 1:23). Scholars such as Don Thorsen (2020) emphasize that "Emmanuel" lies at the core of the Christian covenant, underscoring God's unchanging commitment to remain present with those who call upon Him. This promise transcends the notion of mere proximity, representing an eternal dedication and an active presence in both moments of rejoicing and times of trial.

Connection Between the Old Testament Covenant and Jesus as Emmanuel

The Old Testament covenant, symbolized by the Ark of the Covenant, embodied God's promises and His enduring presence among His people. Theologian Gayraud S. Wilmore (1983) observes that the divine presence in the Ark foreshadows the ultimate closeness of God with His people in Emmanuel. This relationship between the Ark and Christ illustrates a continuous thread of divine commitment. While the Ark served as a tangible reminder of God's covenant, Jesus embodies the fulfillment of that promise, manifesting God's presence in a personal and life-altering manner. Through Emmanuel, God's promise transitions from a sacred symbol to a living reality, deepening the connection between the divine and humanity.

Understanding "God with Us" as a Covenant Promise

The phrase "God with us" represents a promise of closeness, shared life, and common purpose. It reassures believers that God is always with them, no matter the circumstances, fostering a strong and personal relationship. In challenging times, the Black Church has embraced Emmanuel as a powerful reminder that God's presence remains through every trial. In every worship service, every gospel song, and every act of community care, the Black Church demonstrates the reality of "God with us." This isn't just an abstract idea but a real, sustaining force in everyday life (Wilmore, 1983). Living out Emmanuel highlights a covenant that not only promises God's presence but also actively supports believers in their faith.

Symbolism of the Ark of the Covenant and Its Connection to Emmanuel

Role of the Ark in Representing God's Presence

In ancient Israel, the Ark of the Covenant was much more than a sacred object; it was seen as the home of God's presence among His people. Placed in the Holy of Holies, the Ark was a clear sign of God's closeness and active involvement in their lives. It traveled with the Israelites through the wilderness and into battles, constantly reminding them that God was with them not only during worship but also in times of hardship and victory. The Ark's role as a symbol of God's presence points forward to a greater revelation: Emmanuel. The Ark anticipates a time where God would not only dwell symbolically but would also take on flesh so that He could fully dwell among His people.

The Incarnation as the Fulfillment of the Ark's Symbolism

Jesus Christ brings the promise of the Ark to life in a profound way. The items inside the Ark—the tablets (God's Law), Aaron's rod (God's chosen leadership), and manna (spiritual nourishment)—all find their true meaning in Jesus. He fulfills the Law by living out its teachings with perfect love and justice. As the ultimate leader, Jesus guides humanity through His example of sacrificial love. Additionally, He is the Bread of Life, providing spiritual sustenance that nourishes both body and soul.

In Emmanuel, the Ark's symbolism is fulfilled when God's promise becomes a living, breathing reality. Moving from the Ark to Jesus marks a significant change in the relationship between God and His people. Unlike the Ark, which was kept in a specific place and accessible only to a few, Jesus's presence is available to everyone, everywhere. This change highlights the New Covenant's inclusive nature, where God's presence is no longer confined to sacred objects but lives within the hearts of believers and the community of the Church.

Emmanuel and the Church as the New Dwelling Place

With Emmanuel, the Black Church finds a deep and meaningful connection to God's presence. As a community of faith, the Church carries forward the Ark's legacy of God walking alongside His people. It acts as both a safe haven and a vessel, reminding those who are marginalized that God's promise to be with them remains steadfast through every challenge and triumph. Just as the Ark was central to Israel's identity and worship, the Church upholds the reality of Emmanuel, showing that God's presence is active, dynamic, and deeply involved in the lives of His people.

This connection emphasizes the ongoing relationship between the Ark's symbolism and the mission of the Black Church. Both highlight a God who is not distant but actively lives among His people, guiding them toward freedom, justice, and hope. By embracing Emmanuel, the Black Church not only honors the legacy of the Ark but also reinterprets it within the New Covenant, ensuring that God's promise of presence and support continues to inspire and sustain each generation.

Role of the Black Church as a Continuation of God's Promise

Black Church as the Modern Ark, a Living Testament of Covenant

Like the Ark of the Covenant, which symbolized God's presence during Israel's wilderness journey, the Black Church has upheld God's divine presence through the "wilderness" of history. From slavery and segregation to ongoing struggles against systemic oppression, the Black Church has been a living testament to God's covenant.

This parallel highlights the Church's role as a modern vessel of God's promises, embodying His presence in the lives of African Americans. As the spiritual and cultural continuation of God's covenant, the Black Church inhabits a unique place, providing fortitude, hope, and divine companionship to a marginalized community.

Beyond a religious institution, the Black Church serves as a sacred repository of faith and identity, carrying God's promises through history's trials and triumphs, demonstrating that God's covenant extends beyond a single moment or artifact, continually unfolding in the lives of His people.

As a "modern Ark," the Black Church bears the responsibility to sustain faith, advocate for justice, and nurture resilience, ensuring that God's covenant remains active and visible. Through worship, activism, and commitment, the Black Church affirms that God's presence is alive, dynamic, and active in every era.

Historical Role in Preserving Faith and Community

The Black Church has been the cornerstone of the African American community, preserving faith, culture, and identity across generations. Like the Ark of the Covenant, which symbolized God's promises to the Israelites, the Black Church has journeyed with its members, embodying faith, collective memory, and endurance.

Beyond worship, the Church serves as a shelter where stories of struggle and triumph are shared, maintaining the community's spiritual and cultural identity. Through hymns, sermons, and social services, the Black Church reflects God's faithfulness and stands as a living testament to Emmanuel—God with us. These practices foster hope and strength in the face of adversity (Grigsby, 2021).

Bridging the Old and New Testaments
Through Covenant

The Black Church serves as a powerful bridge, linking the covenantal themes of the Old Testament with their ultimate fulfillment in the New Testament through Christ. It embodies the promise of Emmanuel—God's enduring presence and commitment to His people. Through its theology, worship, and activism, the Black Church weaves together the narrative of God's covenant, creating a living testimony that connects the divine promises of the past with their life-changing impact on the present.

By emphasizing Emmanuel, the Church not only recalls the symbolic significance of the Ark of the Covenant but also reaffirms that God's promises are active and relevant today. It serves as a reminder that God is not distant; He is present in every struggle and triumph, working through faith communities to bring liberation, justice, and hope. The Black Church's ability to anchor itself in this covenantal continuity ensures its role as both a preserver of tradition and a harbinger of spiritual renewal in the modern age.

With Us: The Incarnation as a
Model of Divine Presence

The name "Emmanuel" reveals the very essence of God's mission: to be intimately "with us." Through the Incarnation, God chose not only to watch over humanity but to step directly into human history, experiencing life's joys and sorrows alongside His creation. As John 1:14 (*New King James Version*, 1982) states, "the Word became flesh and dwelt among us," a powerful image that encapsulates God's desire to be near His people. This is not just a theological concept; it is the heart of the Christian faith—God's declaration of continual presence, a divine accompaniment through every chapter of human existence. As I wrote in "Joy to the World" (Richardson, 2006b), "In the coming of Jesus, God made a decisive declaration: He is with us, in the joy and in the struggle."

The Black Church has uniquely embodied this concept of "Emmanuel." In its worship, fellowship, and activism, the Church testifies to God's continuous presence. From the whispered prayers of enslaved Africans seeking comfort to the passionate sermons that galvanized the Civil Rights Movement, the Black Church has carried forward the message of Emmanuel. This divine companionship—God with us—has been a wellspring of hope for Black communities throughout history. As theologians like Gayraud S. Wilmore (1998) and Katie G. Cannon (1988) have observed, the Black Church has been a spiritual and social force, fostering fortitude and unity in the face of systemic oppression. This experience of God being "with us" is made visible in how the Church nurtures hope, unity, and purpose, even in the most challenging times.

Understanding "With Us" in the Context of Jesus's Ministry

In his sermon "The Only Route to Heaven," Sandy F. Ray shares an experience in a small Mississippi town where a single, dangerous bus route was his only way home. He likens this challenging journey to a spiritual truth, saying, "the jungle is the only route to the Promised Land" (Ray, 1967, pp. 28–29). This memorable image reflects the way the Black Church upholds Jesus's promise to be near, much like the Ark of the Covenant once represented God's guiding presence for the Israelites. As Ray depended on that one route to get home, the Black Church has provided generations of Black Americans with a secure path through life's struggles, offering hope and strength along the way.

Ray's "jungle" is not simply a figure of speech; it highlights very real obstacles such as systemic injustice, economic pressures, and discrimination—what he calls the "handicaps and horrors" of life (Ray, 1967, pp. 28–29). Still, the Church echoes Jesus's own reassurance: "Be not afraid, I am with thee." Through sermons, music, and fellowship, Black preachers affirm that the Church is both a spiritual foundation and a source of community support. This focus mirrors Jesus's ministry, where He walked beside those on the margins, providing guidance, healing, and a constant reminder that God is truly with us.

By emphasizing Jesus's promise to stay close, the Black Church serves as both a route and a refuge, drawing believers together to face spiritual and social challenges. It functions as a covenant community, offering direction and confidence in times of hardship. Grounded in the Incarnation's promise, the Church continues Jesus's commitment to walk with His people in every circumstance.

Jesus as the Embodiment of God's Presence Among Humanity

Jesus's ministry was a living example of God's "with us" mission. Every act of healing, every word of comfort, and every moment spent among the marginalized represented God's profound commitment to His people. Theologian Dietrich Bonhoeffer (1949) emphasized that the Incarnation was God's ultimate statement of solidarity, His choice to be with humanity not only in spirit but also in shared experience. Jesus did not remain distant or aloof; He entered into the lives of the people, sharing their burdens, joys, and struggles. In this way, He became the embodiment of divine companionship, a reminder that God's presence is accessible and personal.

"With Us" in Jesus's Acts of Healing and Compassion

In the Gospels, Jesus consistently demonstrated what it means for God to be "with us" through acts of healing and compassion. When Jesus touched lepers, restored sight to the blind, and fed the hungry, He was not only addressing physical needs but also affirming God's presence among those who felt most abandoned. Each miracle was an invitation to experience God's love palpably, to feel His compassion in the midst of suffering. In Jesus's ministry, the companionship of "with us" took on tangible meaning as He healed and restored those in need (Grigsby, 2021). This compassionate presence is mirrored in the mission of the Black Church, which continually seeks to alleviate the burdens of its community through both spiritual and practical support.

Solidarity With the Oppressed and Marginalized

Jesus's commitment to those on the margins—tax collectors, prostitutes, the poor—demonstrated radical inclusivity. He did not merely observe the suffering of the oppressed; He actively stood with them, advocating for justice and dignity. This solidarity with the marginalized resonates deeply within the Black Church, which has long aligned itself with the mission of "God with us" by standing with the oppressed.

The Black Church as an Embodiment of Emmanuel

In *Black Church/White Theology*, Rev. Dr. Theron Williams (2022) describes the "Domination System" as a social structure designed to protect privilege by keeping marginalized communities at the bottom. This system doesn't just exist; it thrives in ways that reinforce systemic inequality, creating steep challenges for the Black community. Against this backdrop, the Black Church has stepped in as a powerful counterforce. Much like the Ark of the Covenant symbolized God's presence and protection for the Israelites, the Black Church has carried forward God's promises, offering spiritual refuge and a voice for justice.

The Black Church's role as both refuge and advocate reflects its mission to meet more than just spiritual needs. It takes on the mantle of addressing systemic injustice while providing hope and community. Williams likens the Church to a sacred guide that helps people navigate life's challenges with perseverance and purpose. Just as the Ark journeyed with the Israelites, the Black Church journeys with its community, bringing unity and determination to the struggle against injustice.

Williams also highlights how movements like Black theology and womanist theology emerge from real-life experiences of oppression. These are not just ideas discussed in seminaries; they are practical, lived expressions of faith. Cannon (1988) describes womanist theology as a survival tool that affirms the experiences and spirituality of Black women. We will examine these theological approaches in more detail in later chapters. By embracing these theological approaches, the Black Church expands its message of liberation, creating a space where everyone, especially those on the margins, can find belonging and dignity.

One of the defining features of the Black Church is how it reinterprets the gospel. While white evangelicalism often focuses on personal salvation, the Black Church weaves spiritual salvation with social liberation. Williams (2022) tells the story of a pastor who once viewed the gospel through an individualistic lens, focused solely on personal sin and redemption. Over time, this pastor came to embrace the Church's broader vision: a gospel that speaks to collective struggles and the promise of liberation for all. This vision aligns with the Ark's role as a symbol of God's enduring faithfulness, reminding the community that they are never alone in their fight for justice.

The Black Church serves a dual role in leading cultural and social transformation (Wilmore, 1998). The Church isn't just a place to worship on Sundays; it's where faith meets action, where the community organizes to address pressing issues like systemic racism, economic disparity, and educational inequality. This is what makes the Church such a vital institution. It doesn't just talk about hope and liberation; it lives them.

Through its advocacy and spiritual guidance, the Black Church continues to serve as a modern-day Ark. It holds the community's collective stories, offers strength in the face of adversity, and reminds its members that God's promises remain steadfast. It's a place where tradition meets transformation, ensuring that faith, justice, and love remain at the heart of the Black experience.

Collective Worship as a Manifestation of God's Presence

In the communal gatherings of the Black Church, God's presence is made manifest. When congregants join together in song, prayer, and worship, they are not only expressing individual faith but experiencing a collective encounter with Emmanuel. The sanctuary becomes a place where the divine and human intersect, where every voice raised in gospel hymns resonates with the power of God's presence. This experience is particularly powerful within the Black Church, where worship is not a passive ritual but an active encounter. Worship is the full embodiment of Emmanuel, God in our midst (Bonhoeffer, 1949). This embodied experience perfectly encapsulates the vibrancy of Black Church worship.

Social Action and Advocacy as Expressions of Emmanuel

The Black Church has not confined its mission to the walls of its buildings; it extends "God with us" into the streets, workplaces, and political arenas. From the abolitionist era to the Civil Rights Movement and beyond, the Black Church has actively participated in the fight for justice. Social action within the Black Church is more than mere activism; it is a theological response, a continuation of Jesus's mission to uplift the oppressed and advocate for the marginalized.

The Black Church's mission embodies God's promise to be with His people, especially in struggle. In this way, the Black Church becomes a vessel of Emmanuel, a physical manifestation of God's commitment to justice.

Building Communal Resilience and Unity

One of the most powerful aspects of "God with us" in the Black Church is the sense of unity and resilience it fosters. When faced with adversity, the Black Church provides not only spiritual encouragement but also a practical support system that sustains individuals through difficult times. This community-centered approach reflects the heart of Emmanuel. Wilmore (1998) highlights how the Black Church's robustness speaks to God's steadfast presence. Through shared worship, social action, and mutual support, the Black Church lives out the mission of Emmanuel, God with us, in every challenge.

Manifesting Divine Presence Through Worship and Community

Role of Collective Worship in Experiencing "God with Us"

Worship within the Black Church is a beautiful, collective encounter with God. Each worship service is a reminder that God is not only present but actively involved in the lives of His people. The communal aspect of Black Church worship allows believers to share in the experience of Emmanuel, reinforcing the reality that God's presence is with them in a unique, powerful way. Every song sung and every prayer offered invites God's nearness, creating an atmosphere where faith is both celebrated and strengthened.

Gospel Music and Testimonies as Expressions of Shared Faith

Gospel music, with its rich heritage and emotional depth, is central to the worship experience in the Black Church. Songs of praise, lament, and hope serve as communal prayers, uniting the congregation in shared expression and reaffirming God's presence. Testimonies, too, play a vital role, as individuals share personal experiences of God's intervention and grace. Through gospel music and testimonies, the Black Church offers a space where members can experience "God with us," not just as a theological truth but as a lived reality that touches each person's life.

Worship Practices as Daily Reminders of Divine Companionship

Beyond the safe haven, the Black Church instills in its members a sense of God's companionship in everyday life. Prayer meetings, Bible studies, and fellowship gatherings extend the experience of "God with us" into the daily routines of believers. These practices reinforce the message that God's presence is not limited to a single event but is a continuous support, guiding and uplifting them in all aspects of life. This constant awareness of God's presence strengthens the community, reminding each person that, as Emmanuel, God is with them in every moment, providing solace and strength.

For Us: God's Advocacy and the Mission of the Black Church

The life, death, and resurrection of Jesus Christ reveal God as fundamentally "for us." Romans 8:31 states, "If God is for us, who can be against us?" This declaration goes beyond encouragement; it speaks to the divine advocacy that God demonstrated by sending Jesus to stand in humanity's place, offering Himself as the ultimate sacrifice for reconciliation and redemption. Through His atoning work, Jesus embodied God's desire to actively work for the good of His people. This redemptive mission has deep implications for the Black Church, which has long embraced the role of advocate and protector for its community. The Black Church has become, in essence, an extension of God's advocacy. James Cone and Gayraud Wilmore (1979) wrote, "the Church is that people called into being by the power and love of God to share in his revolutionary activity for the liberation of man" (p. 78).

The Atoning Work of Christ and Its Implications for Advocacy

The Cross as God's Ultimate Act of Advocacy and Love

The Cross is central to understanding God's advocacy and love for humanity. As John Stott (1986) explains, the Cross represents the ultimate act of advocacy because "through Christ crucified, God substituted himself for us and bore our sins, dying in our place the death we deserved to die, in order that we might be restored to his favor and adopted into his family" (p. 13). Christ was the epitome of advocating for us sinners.

Theologian Alister McGrath (1996) further emphasizes that the Cross is God's way of standing in the gap for those who could not stand for themselves—a message that resonates deeply within the Black Church's mission. The sacrificial love displayed on the Cross is mirrored in the Church's work to stand in the gap for those marginalized by society, becoming advocates for justice, dignity, and equality.

Black Liberation Theology and the Call for Social Justice

Black liberation theology, as articulated by scholars such as James H. Cone (1975), builds on the notion that God is not indifferent to oppression but actively seeks justice for the oppressed. This theological perspective asserts that the Black Church is called to follow Christ's example on the Cross, advocating for social justice as an integral part of its mission. The Black Church, much like Jesus, stands with and for the oppressed, serving as a prophetic voice against the injustices of the world. This call for social justice is not only a reflection of God's advocacy but also an essential expression of the Church's identity.

Role of Atonement in Inspiring the Church's Mission

The atonement, as theologians like Stott (1986) argue, is foundational to the Church's mission to defend dignity and justice. The Cross, symbolizing God's unyielding love and advocacy, serves as a continual reminder that the Church must champion the well-being of its community. This commitment to advocacy, inspired by the atoning work of Christ, manifests in the Church's dedication to providing spiritual guidance, practical support, and a place of refuge for those in need. The Black Church embodies the message of the Cross, where divine love meets human suffering and works for transformation.

The Black Church as a Champion for Justice and Dignity

Advocacy During the Civil Rights Movement

During the Civil Rights Movement, the Black Church was a source of hope and a force for social change, a role it undertook with a sense of divine mission. The Civil Rights Movement underscored the Church's identity as an institution "for us," advocating tirelessly for the rights of Black Americans and standing against injustice. This role as a champion for dignity reflects the very essence of Emmanuel: God working through His Church for the well-being of His people.

Education, Economic Empowerment, and Community Initiatives

The Black Church has long understood that God's advocacy extends beyond spiritual matters, encompassing all aspects of life. As such, it has committed to empowering its community through education, economic initiatives, and community programs that promote social mobility and stability. This commitment has historical roots, where churches provided schooling, vocational training, and financial aid to uplift the community. By advocating for education and economic empowerment, the Black Church echoes the message of "God for us," striving to remove barriers and create opportunities for growth and prosperity.

Contemporary Social Justice Efforts as Reflections of Emmanuel

Today, the Black Church continues to address systemic injustices, recognizing that God's love compels it to be actively involved in issues affecting its people. From initiatives aimed at combating racial discrimination to programs addressing housing inequality, the Black Church remains a vital advocate for justice. This ongoing mission reflects the belief that God is actively working through the Church, bringing Emmanuel—"God with us"—into every social, economic, and political realm. Through these efforts, the Black Church reaffirms its role as an oasis of advocacy, where divine love and justice intersect.

Community Advocacy: Education, Economic Empowerment, and Social Justice

Historical Role in Uplifting Black Communities

Historically, the Black Church has been a cornerstone for community support and advancement. During Reconstruction, the Church played a critical role in establishing schools, hospitals, and mutual aid societies to uplift Black communities in a racially hostile environment. This work provided foundational support for the newly emancipated and demonstrated the Church's commitment to advocating for the community's overall well-being. The Black Church's historical role as a pillar of support exemplifies its mission to be "for us"—a proactive source of hope and assistance, drawing from God's promise to care for His people.

Present-Day Programs and Initiatives for Empowerment

Today, the Black Church continues this legacy through modern-day initiatives focused on social and economic empowerment. Churches sponsor programs for youth mentorship, job training, financial literacy, and higher education scholarships. These initiatives are designed to address structural disparities and provide pathways to success, ensuring that the community has the tools it needs to thrive. In doing so, the Black Church fulfills its role as a champion for progress, reminding its members that, just as God is for them, the Church is committed to their personal and collective advancement.

Long-Term Vision for Uplifting Future Generations

The Black Church's advocacy is not confined to the present; it also encompasses a vision for future generations. By investing in education, mentorship, and community development, the Church lays a foundation for continued empowerment and success. This long-term vision reflects a commitment to sustain the mission of "God for us," ensuring that future generations have the resources, support, and faith needed to navigate life's challenges. In preparing young leaders and fostering resilience, the Black Church embodies a divine foresight that seeks not only immediate change but enduring transformation.

As Us: Jesus's Humanity and the Church's Incarnational Mission

In becoming human, Jesus signified that God came "as us," fully embracing the human experience in all its complexity. The Incarnation reveals a profound act of solidarity, where God enters the world not merely to observe but to participate, to feel, and to suffer alongside humanity. Hebrews 2:14–18 (*New King James Version*, 1982) captures this concept, noting that Christ "shared in [our] humanity," experiencing hunger, sorrow, joy, and even death. Theologians such as Dietrich Bonhoeffer (1949) and Raymond Brown (1994) argue that the Incarnation is foundational to understanding God's solidarity with humanity, as it shows that God is not a distant observer but a close companion in life's struggles. This idea that God came "as us" forms the core of the Black Church's mission and identity, as the Church embodies the shared struggles of its community, standing as a powerful representation of divine empathy and solidarity.

Theological Significance of Jesus as Fully Human

Incarnation as a Reflection of Divine Solidarity

The Incarnation represents God's willingness to partake in human limitations and sufferings. Jesus's birth is an act of solidarity with humanity, demonstrating that God does not merely sympathize with our struggles but fully participates in them. Jesus's life, from His humble birth to His suffering on the Cross, illustrates a God who understands human frailty and challenges on an intimate level. This solidarity is particularly significant for communities facing systemic oppression, as it confirms that God does not stand apart from suffering but enters into it with profound empathy.

Experiencing Humanity: Hunger, Sorrow, Joy, and Death

Jesus's earthly life encompassed all aspects of the human condition, including hunger, sorrow, joy, and death. In these experiences, Christ demonstrated that God knows what it is to endure life's hardships. He did not shield Himself from human suffering; rather, He encountered it directly, showing a divine willingness to endure what humanity endures. This aspect of Jesus's life has been central to the Black Church, where each worship service becomes a space to collectively acknowledge and navigate shared pain, much like Jesus did in His ministry. This experience of divine solidarity provides hope and comfort, as it assures believers that God is not detached from their reality but fully understands and participates in their journey.

The Black Church as a Space of Shared Struggle and Divine Empathy

For centuries, the Black Church has been a haven of solidarity and a vessel of divine empathy, where the individual and collective experiences of Black people are honored, uplifted, and given sacred significance. Much like the life and teachings of Jesus, which reflect God's solidarity with humanity, the Black Church embodies this solidarity within its walls, offering a space where every struggle, every sorrow, and every joy finds a place in the community's collective story. Theologian Delores S. Williams (1993) captures this essence, arguing that the shared experiences of suffering and perseverance are central to Black liberation theology. In this theology, the Church is not merely a gathering place but a sacred home where the struggles and triumphs of Black life are held and transformed. The Church becomes a living testimony to God's understanding of human hardship, where pain is neither dismissed nor forgotten but seen as a meaningful aspect of spiritual life.

The Black Church as a Sanctuary of Collective Suffering and Resilience

The Black Church has always been a safe haven where the community can heal from the deep wounds of oppression. It is a place where congregants do not have to mask their pain, where tears and laughter flow freely, as both are seen as integral to the journey of faith. Theologian Delores S. Williams (1993) notes that the Black Church has been a place where the deep wounds of oppression are not ignored but are held and healed in the embrace of a community grounded in shared faith and resilience. Here, sorrow and joy coexist, symbolizing the strength of a people who have faced unimaginable adversities yet continue to rise, supported by their faith and each other.

This resilience is evident in the way the Church encourages the community to lean on one another. In the Black Church, suffering is understood as a collective experience. The struggles of individuals become a shared struggle that is woven into the larger fabric of the Church's spiritual life. Each story of hardship becomes part of the Church's tapestry, allowing congregants to find solace in shared experiences, where burdens are collectively borne, and resilience is cultivated. The love of Christ, which is not merely preached but embodied in each act of compassion, allows the Church to represent God's enduring empathy and solidarity with the oppressed.

Affirming Dignity Amid Systemic Oppression

In a society where systemic racism and economic injustice persist as barriers to dignity and equality, the Black Church stands as a visible embodiment of God's empathy, providing a space where every individual's worth is affirmed and defended. This mission of the Church goes beyond providing spiritual refuge; it fosters a tangible environment of solidarity, compassion, and perseverance. Following Jesus's example, who "came as us" and affirmed the dignity of the marginalized, the Church embraces its role in advocating for justice and equality (D. Williams, 1993). This alignment with Jesus's solidarity with the oppressed provides a theological foundation for the Black Church's ongoing mission to fight for justice.

The Church's staying power lies in its unchanging commitment to affirm the worth of each congregant and to stand with those who face daily battles against injustice. "The [B]lack [C]hurch must maintain its inherited legacy of the Old Testament as a liberating influence with a divine agenda if it is to once again function as a liberating institution within unjust human systems that still seek to enslave " (J. Taylor, 2020, p. 62). By embracing this mission, the Church transforms sorrow into hope and indignation into a call for change, reinforcing the belief that every life within the community holds intrinsic value and divine purpose.

Never Left Us: The Enduring Presence of the Black Church

The promise of Jesus to never leave nor forsake His followers, as recorded in Matthew 28:20 (*New King James Version*, 1982), is a profound assurance of God's eternal presence. This promise, woven through the history of the Black Church, serves as a powerful foundation for perseverance and hope. The Black Church has become an enduring symbol of this divine promise, a constant reminder to its members that God's presence is unfaltering, even in life's darkest valleys.

Historical Role of the Black Church as a Place of Refuge

Providing Solace During Slavery and the Civil Rights Era

The Black Church's role as a place of refuge began during the era of slavery, when it became a sacred haven for the enslaved. In those times, the Church was often the only space where Black individuals could experience a sense of dignity and humanity, and it provided an environment where they could connect with a God who understood their suffering. Wilmore (1983) describes how, in hidden gatherings, enslaved people found a spiritual homeland that reminded them of their intrinsic worth. These early worship services became expressions of resistance, hope, and a deep belief in God's promise to never abandon His people.

During the Civil Rights Era, the Black Church again became a place of refuge, this time as an organizing ground for marches, sit-ins, and nonviolent protests. The Church provided not only spiritual support but also practical resources for those fighting for justice. It was within these church walls that leaders like Rosa Parks, John Lewis, Fannie Lou Hamer, Ella Baker, and Fred Shuttlesworth found the strength to advocate for civil rights, relying on the Church's ability to inspire resilience and remind its congregants that God had never left us (Cone, 1975). This legacy of refuge continues today, as the Black Church remains a vital source of strength and comfort in the fight for equality.

The Church as a Safe Haven Amid Societal Oppression

Throughout history, the Black Church has consistently served as a shelter from societal oppression, offering a place where believers could retreat from the discrimination and violence they faced in the outside world. It was in the Church that individuals felt safe, heard, and valued— qualities that were often denied to them in society. This safe haven allowed Black communities to process their pain, find strength in shared faith, and draw courage from each other's experiences. Even in contemporary times, as racial tensions persist, the Black Church continues to be a safe space, affirming the value of Black lives and providing an environment where hope and perseverance can flourish.

Legacy as a Shelter for the Spiritually and Socially Oppressed

The Black Church's legacy as a shelter for the oppressed extends beyond physical protection; it includes spiritual support for those marginalized by society. This role helps fulfill God's promise to never leave His people. By offering refuge and advocacy for the spiritually and socially oppressed, the Black Church has carved out a unique identity as a source of hope and empowerment. The Church's commitment to providing refuge springs from the foundational belief that God's love and presence endure through all of life's challenges, cementing its legacy as a place of comfort and empowerment.

Community Resilience and Hope Through the Black Church

Spiritual Support During Collective Hardships and Triumphs

The Black Church's role as a support system is especially evident during times of communal hardship, such as economic downturns, natural disasters, and acts of violence. In these moments, the Church becomes a unifying force, drawing on collective faith to offer strength and comfort. Congregants gather to pray, sing, and uplift each other, reinforcing their shared resilience. The Black Church became the cutting edge of the freedom movement throughout most of the 19th century by helping its members turn hardships into opportunities for unity and strength (Wilmore, 1983). This resilience is not just for survival but also for triumph. The Church celebrates victories, large and small, as reflections of God's faithfulness.

Long-Lasting Impact on Generational Faith and Resilience

The impact of the Black Church on generational faith cannot be overstated. Through the Church, each generation learns to navigate adversity with a spirit of hope, knowing that God's promise to never leave us extends across time. Parents, grandparents, and elders pass down stories of how faith sustained them, instilling in younger generations the same confidence in God's presence. This generational resilience, cultivated within the Church, ensures that faith remains a constant, empowering future generations to face life's challenges with strength and courage.

Coming Back to Get Us: Eschatological Hope in the Black Church

The eschatological hope of Christ's return, described in 1 Thessalonians 4:16–17 (*New King James Version*, 1982), underscores a core belief within Christianity: that God is indeed "coming back to get us." This hope has been a true source of strength within the Black Church, reminding believers that their struggles are temporary and that God's promise of ultimate justice, peace, and restoration remains steadfast. Theologians such as Jürgen Moltmann (1967) and Wolfhart Pannenberg (1991) argue that the Second Coming is the culmination of God's promise to humanity, when all wrongs will be set right, and divine justice will prevail. This hope is more than a theological concept; it is a sustaining force, encouraging believers to persevere knowing that their faith is not in vain.

Theology of Christ's Return and Its Hope for Justice

Christ's Return as the Fulfillment of God's Promise to Humanity

The promise of Christ's return represents the ultimate fulfillment of God's covenant with humanity. This promise assures believers that God has not forgotten them and that He will complete His work of restoration. In the Black Church, this eschatological hope resonates deeply, reinforcing the idea that God's justice will prevail over the injustices that have plagued humanity. As Moltmann (1967) emphasizes, the Second Coming is a declaration of God's fidelity. The author wrote how this event "points back to the promises of God and forwards to an eschaton in which his divinity is revealed in all. It must then be understood as the eschatological coming to pass of the faithfulness of God" (p. 177). This truth affirms that the struggles of the present will give way to a future of divine justice and peace. This assurance encourages the Black Church community to remain steadfast in faith, knowing that their present hardships are but a prelude to God's redemptive work.

Eschatological Hope in Black Liberation Theology

Eschatology plays a pivotal role in Black liberation theology, as scholars like Kelly Brown Douglas (1999) argue. For the Black Church, the anticipation of Christ's return is more than a future hope; it is a declaration of God's commitment to justice and equality. This theology encourages the Black Church to envision a future where systemic oppression and suffering are eradicated and replaced by God's divine order. By focusing on Christ's return, the Black Church affirms that justice and liberation are integral to God's plan. This eschatological perspective has fueled the Church's commitment to social justice, as believers work to make visible on earth the justice and peace that will be fully realized in God's kingdom.

Vision of a Future Where Justice, Peace, and Righteousness Prevail

The vision of a world where justice, peace, and righteousness reign has sustained the Black Church through generations. The Second Coming offers a picture of ultimate redemption, a time when the burdens of injustice will be lifted, and the dignity of all people will be restored. This vision aligns with the Black Church's pursuit of equality and justice, reinforcing the belief that God's kingdom is not only a spiritual reality but also a social one, encompassing the total liberation of humanity. This hope gives believers a sense of purpose, motivating them to embody God's justice in their daily lives as they wait for the fulfillment of His promise.

The Black Church's Vision of Future Restoration and Redemption

Eschatological Perspectives on Liberation and Ultimate Justice

For the Black Church, the hope of future restoration is a source of immense strength. This belief in ultimate justice shapes how the Church views liberation, seeing it as both a present struggle and a future certainty. Douglas (1999) explains that this eschatological hope fuels the Black Church's mission, encouraging believers to advocate for justice here and now as a reflection of the coming kingdom. By focusing on this divine promise, the Black Church maintains a hopeful stance, affirming that God's justice will ultimately restore all that has been lost.

Hope for Redemption as a Sustaining Force for the Community

The anticipation of Christ's return serves as a sustaining force for the Black Church community, offering a vision of redemption that uplifts and empowers. This hope has kept the Black Church resilient through adversity, as it reassures congregants that God's commitment to them does not waver. During times of collective hardship, the promise of redemption acts as a spiritual anchor, enabling the Church to continue its mission with confidence. This hope is not passive; it is active, inspiring the Black Church to embody God's love and justice as a foretaste of the redemption that will one day be fully realized.

Preparation and Anticipation for Christ's Return

The Black Church's emphasis on preparing for Christ's return encourages believers to live with intention and purpose. This preparation is not only spiritual but also practical, as the Church calls its members to actively engage in works of justice, compassion, and unity. The anticipation of Christ's return motivates the Black Church to foster a community that embodies the principles of God's kingdom, creating a space where faith and action intersect. This preparation for Christ's return reinforces the Church's mission to be a light in the world, working to establish God's kingdom on earth as it is in heaven.

Sustaining Faith Through Hope of Ultimate Deliverance

Role of Hope in Perseverance Through Trials

The eschatological hope of ultimate deliverance has been a wellspring of perseverance for the Black Church. This hope provides a framework for understanding suffering, allowing believers to see their trials as temporary and to view their faith as a pathway to enduring strength. The promise of ultimate deliverance assures the Black Church community that their struggles are not in vain. By keeping their eyes fixed on the future, members of the Black Church are able to persevere, knowing that God's justice and mercy will ultimately prevail.

Community-Building in Expectation of the Second Coming

The Black Church fosters a sense of community centered around the shared expectation of Christ's return. This expectation builds solidarity among believers, reminding them that they are not alone in their journey. In worship, study, and service, the Black Church cultivates an environment of mutual support, where hope is reinforced through collective faith. This eschatological community-building strengthens the Church's mission, as it provides believers with the support they need to remain steadfast in their walk with God.

Faithfulness and Preparedness in Anticipation of Redemption

The Black Church instills a deep sense of faithfulness and preparedness, urging its members to live in alignment with God's will while anticipating the fulfillment of His promises. This call to faithfulness is not passive; it is an active commitment to embodying justice, mercy, and compassion in everyday life. The Church becomes a space where believers are encouraged to reflect God's kingdom values in their personal actions and communal efforts, making divine promises tangible in the here and now.

This readiness reflects the Church's dual mission: to prepare for Christ's return while addressing present needs and injustices. The Church is not merely a waiting room for heaven but an active participant in the work of redemption on earth. The emphasis on preparedness is woven into the Church's teachings, worship, and activism that creates a community that remains grounded in hope and purpose.

The understanding of Jesus as Emmanuel, "God with us," is central to this mission. Jesus's presence fulfills and expands the symbolism of the Ark of the Covenant, offering more than physical proximity. It represents God's eternal commitment to humanity. This divine companionship is a source of strength in times of celebration and challenge alike, reinforcing the Church's role as both a spiritual guide and a catalyst for social change. Through this lens, faithfulness and preparedness become not only spiritual disciplines but also acts of hope and transformation in anticipation of redemption.

3

The Evolving Practices of the Black Church in the 21st Century

THE 21ST CENTURY PRESENTS THE BLACK CHURCH WITH A unique opportunity: to honor its sacred traditions while embracing the realities of a rapidly changing world. No longer bound solely by brick-and-mortar sanctuaries, the Church now spans digital landscapes, engages in global conversations, and addresses the concerns of a younger, more diverse generation. As technology reshapes worship, and modern social movements demand an evolving theology of justice, the Black Church is reimagining how it serves as both a spiritual refuge and a catalyst for change.

While its historic role as a sanctuary and moral compass remains vital, the Church now faces a landscape that requires innovation alongside tradition. From virtual platforms that connect worshippers across borders to fresh approaches for engaging youth and addressing contemporary issues like mental health, the Black

Church is evolving, crafting new ways to embody its enduring mission.

In this chapter, we explore how the Black Church continues to adapt—through technology, activism, and inclusivity—while maintaining its essential identity. By walking this delicate line between legacy and progress, the Church ensures it remains a relevant, transformative force for generations to come.

For centuries, the Black Church has offered refuge to Black people in times of trial and triumph, serving as a moral compass and a hub for community organization. As a historical anchor, it has been central to education, social justice, and cultural identity. It is the one place where Black Americans have consistently found an affirmation of their dignity and humanity, even amid systemic adversity. Yet, as society changes, the Church must also find new ways to fulfill its role, adapting to meet the spiritual and social needs of today's congregants while remaining true to its roots. This adaptation is both a challenge and a call to action. To remain relevant, the Black Church must walk a fine line, blending the wisdom of the past with the innovation demanded by the future.

In recent years, technology has transformed the way we worship, engage, and sustain our faith. Digital platforms like YouTube, Facebook, and Zoom have become vital tools, bringing church services, prayer meetings, and community gatherings into the homes of congregants across the globe. This shift was especially essential during the COVID-19 pandemic, when physical gatherings were restricted, yet the Church found ways to stay connected.

By embracing digital worship and online community building, the Black Church has extended its reach, breaking down barriers and creating a space where worship is accessible to all.

At the same time, social movements like Black Lives Matter have invigorated the Church's commitment to justice, echoing the activism that fueled the Civil Rights Movement. The Black Church, ever the beacon of advocacy, has renewed its role as both safe haven and agent of social change, organizing for racial justice, equality, and the dismantling of systemic injustice. Today's Black Church is once again speaking truth to power, standing in solidarity with those on the frontlines of social justice battles, and asserting its voice in public and political discourse.

Yet, amid this spirit of innovation and activism, the Church faces new challenges. Younger generations often seek an authentic, experiential connection to faith, one that aligns with their values and lived realities. Many consider themselves "spiritual but not religious," urging the Black Church to address issues such as mental health, economic empowerment, and environmental justice in ways that resonate with modern sensibilities. By embracing these conversations and creating spaces where younger congregants feel seen and valued, the Black Church paves the way for a new era of faith leadership that is inclusive, grounded, and visionary.

As we journey deeper into the 21st century, the Black Church remains a vital institution that not only adapts but leads, nurturing a legacy of faith, justice, and community.

Through this ongoing evolution, it continues to be a source of strength, inspiring generations to carry forward its mission of empowerment and hope. In a world of change, the Black Church endures as a steadfast compass, guiding its people with grace and conviction, ensuring that faith, unity, and fortitude aren't just ideals; they are the vibrant realities of a living, breathing community.

Contemporary Changes Influencing the Black Church

The Black Church, long regarded as a foundation of the African American community, is currently navigating a transformational period influenced by advances in technology, social justice movements, and evolving patterns of religious participation. These forces are reshaping both traditional practices and the modern role of the Black Church.

The Impact of Technology on Worship and Community Engagement

The integration of technology into worship and community engagement has been one of the most remarkable recent shifts for the Black Church, a change that began even before the onset of the global crisis. The COVID-19 pandemic simply accelerated the adoption of digital platforms such as Zoom, YouTube, and Facebook, fundamentally altering how churches engage with their congregants. These platforms allowed the Black Church to extend its reach beyond physical confines, creating virtual worship spaces and redefining what it means to be present in worship. Technology has become a bridge to keep our communities together, even in moments when we cannot physically gather.

Digital Platforms and Virtual Worship

The move to digital platforms has brought worship services into homes and made spiritual gatherings more accessible. This shift represents a significant departure from traditional in-person gatherings, enabling the Church to connect with congregants far beyond its local community. The ability to provide continuity through virtual worship has underscored the idea that the Church's essence is not limited to a physical building but resides in its people and their connections.

Online Giving and Financial Stability

Alongside digital worship, online giving platforms like Givelify and PayPal have been crucial in ensuring the Church's financial stability. Digital giving allows congregants to support their church even in the absence of physical gatherings, representing a modern adaptation of traditional tithing practices. This new approach has provided financial consistency and reinforced the Church's robustness, even in uncertain times.

Global Connection and Community-Building in the Post-Pandemic World

In the post-pandemic world, the virtual reach of the Black Church has allowed for a sense of global community, connecting congregants across borders and creating a unified spiritual space. This new model has fostered collaborations and opened avenues for community-building on a larger scale, expanding the Church's mission in ways that transcend traditional geographic limitations.

Influence of Social Justice Movements

The Black Church's engagement with social justice issues, particularly racial justice movements, has been reinvigorated in recent years. As a historical advocate for equality and civil rights, the Church has always served as both shelter and advocate for African Americans facing systemic oppression. As previously mentioned, recent social movements like Black Lives Matter have renewed this commitment, highlighting the Church's role as both a moral leader and a center for activism. The Church must speak truth to power and stand boldly against injustice, as it has always been called to do.

Programming Initiatives: Voter Registration, Health Equity, and Racial Justice

The Black Church has also expanded its programming to include initiatives focused on voter registration, health equity, and racial justice. These programs underscore the Church's role in community advocacy, ensuring that congregants are equipped to face systemic issues. Through partnerships with local organizations, the Church provides resources that extend beyond spiritual care, supporting holistic empowerment within the community (Daughtry, 2021).

Shifts in Religious Participation Patterns

Changes in religious participation patterns, particularly among younger generations, have also reshaped the Black Church. The younger demographic often identifies as "spiritual but not religious," seeking authentic, value-aligned experiences in their faith journeys. This shift requires the Black Church to adapt traditional engagement methods to better meet the needs of a spiritually diverse congregation. In 2022, I spoke specifically about this: "We must create spaces where our young people see themselves—where their struggles, triumphs, and voices are not only acknowledged but centered" (Richardson, 2022).

Engaging "Spiritual but not Religious" Generations

The challenge of engaging a generation that is less inclined toward formal religious institutions presents a unique opportunity for the Black Church to create spaces that welcome diverse expressions of spirituality. Embracing this shift is essential for the Church to remain relevant and connected to contemporary values and needs.

Reaching Young Adults Through Social Justice, Arts, and Technology

Programs focused on social justice, creative arts, and technology allow the Black Church to connect with younger adults in ways that are relevant and meaningful. By emphasizing engagement through social advocacy and modern expressions of worship, the Church draws younger members who seek purpose-driven faith experiences.

Importance of Physical Gathering and Community Re-establishment

The need to reclaim physical gathering spaces has become paramount in the post-pandemic era. Although virtual platforms did maintain continuity during the pandemic, the value of in-person fellowship—expressed through shared worship, collective singing, and the warmth of community—has proven irreplaceable. I described the significance of this return to physical presence in one of my sermons, and I stand by it today. There is a power in gathering that cannot be fully replicated online.

Lessons From the Pandemic on Gathering and Fellowship

The pandemic underscored the importance of gathering in person, revealing that physical fellowship remains a crucial part of the Black Church experience. Being together in the same space strengthens bonds and fosters a deeper sense of unity, essential for the Church's staying power.

In-Person Worship and Fellowship as Vital Elements of Faith

In-person worship provides a unique spiritual experience that digital platforms cannot fully replicate. The communal nature of faith within the Black Church emphasizes the importance of sharing physical spaces, reinforcing collective worship as a core expression of spiritual identity.

Strengthening Communal Ties as the Foundation of Black Church Unity

The strength of the Black Church lies in its commitment to building lasting connections. Re-establishing communal ties and fostering supportive relationships within the Church community ensures its role as a source of unity, resilience, and spiritual guidance for its congregants (Daughtry, 2021).

In this era of rapid change, the Black Church's mission remains as vital as ever. By adapting to technological advancements, responding to social justice imperatives, and welcoming shifts in religious engagement, the Black Church continues to be a sacred vessel for the African American community, offering refuge, empowerment, and spiritual sustenance across generations.

Black preachers stand as pillars within the Black Church, holding a sacred role that parallels the Ark of the Covenant's function as a spiritual anchor and a vessel of divine guidance. Much like the Ark, which represented God's enduring covenant with the Israelites, Black preachers are custodians of a sacred commitment to their congregations. This covenant transcends traditional religious duties, encompassing the responsibility to uplift, empower, and provide spiritual leadership in the face of systemic oppression and communal challenges. Their sermons are not merely religious discourses; they are messages of hope, resilience, and justice that affirm the covenantal promise of both spiritual sustenance and temporal deliverance (Wilmore, 1983; G. Taylor, 1977).

Rev. Dr. Gardner C. Taylor, in *How Shall They Preach*, captures the immense responsibility of Black preachers, emphasizing the delicate balance between preparation and inspiration in crafting sermons that nourish the soul and address real-world struggles (G. Taylor, 1977). In this way, Black preachers function much like the Ark—offering shelter within a framework of shared belief and collective purpose. They engage deeply with Scripture, interpreting it not only as a source of theological truths but also as a wellspring of liberation and endurance. Their words resonate deeply with congregants, reflecting the lived experiences of communities navigating oppression while drawing strength from their faith (T. Williams, 2022).

Beyond the pulpit, Black preachers embody the Ark's symbolic role as a bridge between the divine and the community. Their sermons serve as vehicles for divine justice and protection, fortifying the Black Church's mission as both a haven and a catalyst for social action. Through their leadership, Black preachers ensure that the Church remains a guiding light in the ongoing fight for equality and justice, infusing their congregations with the courage needed to face contemporary challenges.

In many ways, Black preachers are not only spiritual leaders but also guardians of a divine promise. They carry the weight of the covenant, ensuring that the Black Church continues to serve as a refuge of faith and a force for change. Their role extends far beyond weekly worship, encompassing advocacy, community building, and the embodiment of divine purpose. As vessels of God's intention, Black preachers keep the covenant alive, anchoring their communities in faith while charting a course toward justice, solidarity, and hope.

Case Study: Grace Baptist Church— A Pivot in the Pandemic

Grace Baptist Church, under my leadership, serves as a compelling example of the Black Church's fortitude and adaptability in navigating the unexpected shifts of the 21st century. The COVID-19 pandemic presented unprecedented challenges, requiring us to reimagine how we minister to, connect with, and nurture our community in a world where in-person gatherings were no longer possible. This moment became a test of our ability to maintain the core of our mission to provide spiritual support, foster connection, and be a steadfast presence—even when our traditional ways of gathering were disrupted.

Embracing Digital Transformation

With in-person services suspended, Grace Baptist pivoted swiftly, embracing technology and digital platforms to continue our ministry. This shift was not without its challenges; it required us to rethink the very nature of communal worship. Could the Church, an entity so deeply rooted in physical gatherings and shared space, still foster connection and spiritual growth in a virtual setting?

As I shared with the congregation during a 2021 sermon, "The pandemic forced us to reimagine what it means to be the Church ... the Church is not confined to a building; it is the people, and we must go where the people are, even if that means going online" (Richardson, 2021). This realization prompted us to leverage online services and virtual fellowship groups, reaching not only our immediate congregation but also members who had relocated or could not physically attend church, expanding our ministry's reach beyond geographical limitations.

Expanding Ministry Offerings: Virtual Fellowship and Support

Recognizing the isolation and uncertainty many faced, we introduced a range of virtual services to nurture the spiritual and emotional well-being of our congregation. Weekly online Bible study sessions, prayer meetings, and counseling services became vital components of our ministry. These offerings allowed us to sustain a rhythm of communal worship and spiritual growth, affirming the Church's presence in people's lives during a time when physical gathering was not possible.

To maintain a sense of fellowship, we hosted virtual community events, including talent shows, discussion panels, and even shared meals via video calls, where congregants gathered online to enjoy a meal together. These gatherings helped sustain a sense of connection and belonging, reminding us that our community extends beyond the walls of the church. Additionally, we strengthened our commitment to personal connection by assigning each deacon to a small group of members. Each deacon was responsible for reaching out regularly to ensure every individual felt supported, heard, and valued.

I personally called members, affirming our commitment to being a church that stands by its people in times of both celebration and trial.

The Hybrid Model: Sustaining Connection Beyond the Pandemic

As restrictions lifted, Grace Baptist adopted a hybrid model, offering both in-person and online services to accommodate a diverse congregation. This approach reflects a broader trend within the Black Church, where congregations in both urban and rural settings have recognized the value of maintaining an online presence. For rural Black churches, where distance can hinder regular attendance, online services have become an essential means of connection. Similarly, some urban congregations have created online-only formats, meeting the needs of those who seek a spiritual home that aligns with their specific circumstances, whether due to mobility challenges, distance, or other personal considerations.

Our commitment to a hybrid model has not only allowed us to retain existing members but has also opened doors to new congregants. By offering multiple avenues to engage—whether through traditional services, online worship, or community outreach initiatives—we have been able to create a more inclusive approach to ministry. This adaptability has broadened our impact, illustrating how the Black Church can evolve to meet contemporary needs while honoring its core mission.

Lessons in Resilience and Adaptability

Grace Baptist's journey during the pandemic underscores the resilience and adaptability that have long defined the Black Church. The challenges faced were not merely logistical but deeply spiritual, requiring us to embrace new forms of ministry while holding fast to our enduring values of compassion, community, and faith. As we navigate an era of rapid social and technological change, the Black Church remains a vital force, committed to providing a safe haven for those in need, offering guidance and support, and adapting in ways that honor both tradition and innovation.

This case study serves as a reminder that while our methods may change, our mission remains constant: to be a stronghold of hope, a source of strength, and a space where every member of our community can find belonging and purpose. Grace Baptist's experience during the pandemic testifies to the life-changing power of faith—a faith that is flexible, responsive, and unaltering in its commitment to serve and uplift Black communities in an ever-changing world.

Initial Challenges and Adaptation to Digital Worship

Navigating the Shift to Online Platforms

The rapid transition to digital worship posed considerable challenges for Black churches, many of which had limited technological infrastructure in place before the pandemic. For congregations unfamiliar with digital tools, the shift required overcoming significant logistical hurdles, including bridging the digital literacy gap among congregants and addressing disparities in access to technology (Hutchings, 2017). The urgency of the pandemic exposed vulnerabilities, as church leaders faced the dual task of selecting user-friendly platforms and swiftly training both staff and congregants to adapt to virtual spaces. This unprecedented pivot to digital worship reshaped our ministry, prompting us to reimagine our traditional approaches and underscoring the flexibility required to uphold our sacred mission in changing times.

Re-Envisioning Worship in the Digital Realm

Adapting worship to a virtual format required a delicate balance of maintaining spiritual depth and fostering community despite physical distance. Our re-envisioned worship included interactive elements such as live chats, communal prayers, and shared music experiences, which invited congregants to participate actively, even from afar. This innovative use of multimedia allowed us to retain the vibrancy and inclusivity that define in-person worship, ensuring that the digital experience resonated deeply and spiritually. We took great care to preserve the sacred rituals of our faith, recognizing that in a time of isolation, these acts of worship could anchor and uplift our community.

Leadership's Role in Technological Adaptation

The role of church leadership was indispensable in navigating this daunting transformation. Pastors, deacons, and other leaders embraced new digital tools with resolve, often learning alongside congregants and demonstrating the adaptability essential for times of change (Hutchings, 2017). By proactively engaging with technology, leaders modeled a steadfast commitment to unity and provided a source of guidance and reassurance. Their efforts reinforced the message that while the nature of our gatherings had shifted, we remained a united community of faith, devoted to one another and to God's mission. This adaptation was a continuation of the Black Church's tradition of leading by example, especially in moments of uncertainty.

Community-Building Efforts During Isolation

Virtual Fellowship as a Remedy for Isolation

Amid the isolation of the pandemic, virtual fellowship events emerged as vital connections, bringing our congregation together in spirit, if not in person. These gatherings—from talent shows to discussion forums— offered congregants a space to share joy, laughter, and support, countering the emotional toll of isolation. Such events were not just forms of entertainment; they became spiritual lifelines, underscoring our commitment to one another. Through these efforts, we demonstrated that our bonds were not confined to physical spaces but strengthened by our collective fortitude as we continued to affirm our unity in faith and fellowship.

The Deacon Board's Essential Role in Maintaining Connection

The deacon board played an instrumental role in sustaining our congregation's sense of community, reaching out to each member with calls and messages of encouragement. These personal touches bridged the divide created by physical separation, ensuring that no member felt isolated or unsupported during this challenging time. I also made it a priority to personally connect with congregants, emphasizing the importance of these relationships and reinforcing the enduring strength of our church family. This proactive and compassionate outreach exemplifies the supportive spirit of the Black Church, serving as a source of comfort, care, and connection when it was most needed.

Online Small Groups as Sustained Support Systems

Throughout the pandemic, our small groups adapted to virtual formats, offering essential support systems that helped congregants stay connected and spiritually grounded. These groups provided safe spaces where members could share their struggles, receive encouragement, and find comfort in each other's presence, even from a distance. By sustaining these support structures, we preserved a sense of community and continuity, underscoring the Black Church's role as a family of faith. These virtual gatherings became reminders that, despite physical separation, we remained a resilient and united body, carrying each other in times of need.

Post-Pandemic Hybrid Model of Worship

Benefits and Challenges of Hybrid Worship

Post-pandemic, we adopted a hybrid worship model that combines in-person and online services to accommodate diverse needs. While hybrid worship offers flexibility and broadens our reach, it also presents challenges, such as balancing engagement for both virtual and in-person attendees. Creating a cohesive experience that serves all participants requires careful planning and a commitment to inclusivity, reflecting the Church's role as a unifying force (Hutchings, 2017).

Engaging Rural and Distant Congregants Through Online-Only Offerings

For members in rural or distant areas, online-only services have become an essential way to stay connected with their church family (Hutchings, 2017). By providing these digital options, Grace Baptist expanded its impact, creating a sense of belonging for those physically far from our location. This approach reflects the adaptability of the Black Church, reaching beyond traditional boundaries to meet the needs of our people, wherever they may be.

The adaptability demonstrated by Grace Baptist Church during the pandemic epitomizes the enduring perseverance of the Black Church. By embracing digital tools, strengthening our community ties, and adopting a hybrid model, we continue to evolve in response to the challenges of the 21st century. Our journey exemplifies how the Black Church remains a safe haven and guiding force for African Americans, affirming that we are not bound by physical walls but united by our shared faith and purpose.

Anchoring the Meaning of the Times

The Black Church has long been a vital interpreter of the cultural and spiritual moment, helping its congregants navigate not only crises but also the everyday complexities of life. Beyond being a refuge, it is a dynamic institution that contextualizes contemporary challenges through the lens of faith and justice. This role requires the Church to do more than hold steady. It calls for active engagement with the evolving realities of its members while keeping its mission rooted in timeless truths.

Rather than simply being an anchor in turbulent times, the Black Church is a guide, offering clarity and inspiration to a community seeking purpose and direction in a rapidly changing world. The Church's ability to synthesize tradition with innovation has made it a spiritual crossroads, where history informs the present and inspires future transformation. Whether through social advocacy, educational initiatives, or culturally relevant worship, the Church serves as a compass, orienting individuals and communities toward a shared vision of hope and empowerment.

By expanding its reach into areas such as mental health, economic empowerment, and digital engagement, the Church ensures that it remains not only relevant but impactful. In this way, it continues to be a vibrant force of progress, balancing reverence for its heritage with a bold embrace of the future.

Addressing Contemporary Issues in Sermons and Programs

Today's sermons increasingly address the issues that shape the lives of Black Americans. The Church tackles topics such as racial injustice, economic hardship, mental health, and social inequalities—offering a spiritual and moral framework that speaks to both timeless and timely concerns. By integrating contemporary social issues into our teachings, we provide ethical guidance that resonates with the real-life struggles of our members (Hutchings, 2017).

Programs focused on social justice have become essential, aligning the Church's mission with the needs of our community (Ransby, 2018). This responsiveness allows the Black Church to address complex modern-day issues without compromising its foundational values. Sermons that confront these challenges help our congregants view faith as both a source of solace and a call to action (Campbell & Tsuria, 2021), strengthening the role of the Black Church as a moral and ethical anchor.

Preaching Social Justice as a Spiritual and Moral Anchor

As previously stated, social justice is woven into the fabric of the Black Church's identity, offering a moral compass in times of societal turbulence (Ransby, 2018). Justice is not separate from the gospel but a core element of our spiritual responsibility, reminding congregants of their duty to uphold equality and fairness. Through justice-centered sermons, we reinforce the Church's historic role as a social and moral guide (Campbell & Tsuria, 2021).

The strength of justice-themed preaching lies in its ability to draw a direct line between biblical teachings and social responsibility. In aligning our faith with the pursuit of justice, we empower the Black Church to stand as a leader in both spiritual and societal domains (Hutchings, 2017). This commitment to justice extends beyond rhetoric; it forms the heart of our mission, underscoring our faith as an agent of change in the broader community.

Empowerment Programs: Aligning Faith With Daily Realities

In his sermon "Wagons Stalled in a Creek," found in *Journeying Through a Jungle*, Sandy F. Ray (1967) offers a vivid picture of the Black Church as a modern Ark of the Covenant—an essential guide for those facing heavy burdens. Ray compares a farmer and his mules pulling wagons out of the mud to the way Black churches, and Black preachers especially, lend crucial support to people weighed down by life's struggles. Through acts of compassion and faith, the Church fulfills a role much like the Ark did for the Israelites, serving as a steadfast protector and guide.

Within the Black Church, preachers bring this supportive vision to life, using faith to lift congregants from despair and help them navigate the muddy roads of adversity (Ray, 1967). Just as the Ark of the Covenant reminded the Israelites of God's faithful presence, the Black Church reassures its members they are not alone, especially in a historical context defined by injustice—an enduring reality Al Sharpton often discusses (Sharpton & Hunger, 2002). In this way, the Black Church stands as a lighthouse of both hope and perseverance, uniting people in solidarity and faith even when life's mud threatens to halt their progress.

Relying on faith and shared support, individuals discover a path forward that echoes the Ark's role as both protector and guide. This collective mission reaffirms the Church's covenantal promise to help people overcome obstacles and move toward healing.

Part of that mission includes empowerment programs that combine spiritual values with real-world resources. Through job training, health advocacy, financial education, and more, the Black Church addresses everyday needs beyond the sanctuary walls (Ransby, 2018). Such initiatives bring biblical teachings into modern life and show how faith can directly impact one's well-being.

By meeting these real-life challenges, empowerment programs remind church members that the Black Church isn't just a place of worship—it's a pillar of community support. This approach strengthens the Church's role as both spiritual haven and practical ally, fostering a holistic support system for all who seek its guidance.

Navigating the Balance Between Tradition and Modernization

Balancing tradition with modernization is a defining characteristic of the Black Church, enabling it to remain robust and relevant in an ever-shifting world. While we hold steadfast to our core values, we also embrace adaptations that allow us to better serve our congregation in contemporary contexts.

Upholding Core Values Amid Societal Shifts

The strength of the Black Church lies in its steadfast commitment to foundational values, even as societal norms and expectations evolve. Our adherence to these core beliefs serves as an anchor, stabilizing our mission through periods of change. By upholding these values, we maintain stability and continuity for our congregation, reaffirming our place as a dependable force in times of uncertainty (Campbell & Tsuria, 2021).

While societal shifts may necessitate new approaches, the Black Church remains grounded in the principles that have guided it since its inception (Ransby, 2018). This steadfastness provides a sense of security for congregants, affirming that our faith and mission are resilient, even in changing times (Hutchings, 2017).

Tradition as Foundation for Addressing Modern Needs

Tradition is not a hindrance but a foundation that allows the Black Church to address modern needs with strength and authenticity. Traditional practices provide a framework that supports our ability to respond to contemporary challenges while honoring our rich historical legacy.

In responding to current issues, we draw on the legacy of past practices to navigate social and spiritual demands effectively. The Church's traditions, deeply rooted in community and resilience, serve as a stabilizing force, allowing us to approach new challenges from a place of strength and unity (Ransby, 2018). This balance of tradition and adaptability ensures that our response to modern issues remains true to our identity (Campbell & Tsuria, 2021).

Balancing Resilience With Adaptability

The Black Church's resilience is complemented by a remarkable adaptability, allowing it to meet modern challenges head-on without compromising its core mission. Adaptability strengthens rather than weakens our foundation, as it empowers the Church to remain a relevant social and spiritual force, meeting congregants where they are.

By balancing tradition with flexibility, we respond to the needs of our community in ways that honor our history while embracing the present. This approach fortifies our role as a steadfast support system, equipping us to serve the spiritual and practical needs of our congregation (Ransby, 2018).

Future Challenges and Opportunities

The Black Church stands at a crucial juncture, facing both challenges and promising opportunities as it seeks to adapt to the needs of a rapidly evolving world. Embracing the future while staying true to its foundational values will be essential. The challenge is not only to remain relevant to younger generations and technologically savvy audiences but also to navigate the larger social and cultural shifts that redefine how people engage with faith and spirituality. These changes offer a unique chance to strengthen the Church's mission, extend its reach, and deepen its impact on both individual lives and the broader community.

Engaging Younger Generations in the Black Church Mission

Adapting Messaging and Methods for Youth Engagement

To engage younger generations effectively, the Black Church must embrace new ways of communicating that resonate with the values and lived experiences of youth. Young people today, described as "spiritual but not religious," often prioritize authenticity, inclusivity, and a sense of social responsibility over formal religious practices (Smith & Snell, 2009; Ransby, 2018). This shift requires churches to adapt their messaging, delivering faith-based lessons that address contemporary social and cultural issues. By speaking to young adults in ways that acknowledge their unique worldview, the Church can create a bridge between tradition and modernity. Emerging adults respond to churches that reflect their concerns and provide a meaningful, relatable experience. The use of social media and digital platforms offers a direct way to reach these audiences, demonstrating that faith can be both enduring and adaptable.

Creating Space for Young Leadership and Involvement

For the Black Church to thrive in the coming decades, it is imperative to cultivate young leaders within the congregation. Empowering youth in leadership roles allows them to see their potential impact, fostering a sense of ownership in the Church's mission (Smith &

Snell, 2009). Creating such spaces not only ensures that the Church remains vibrant and forward-looking but also infuses it with new perspectives and ideas (Campbell & Tsuria, 2021).

Young people bring fresh energy to traditional practices, innovating in ways that keep the Church relevant in a changing world. Ransby (2018) emphasizes that mentoring young leaders and involving them in decision-making processes are critical steps toward continuity. By valuing and nurturing youth contributions, the Black Church can build a legacy that bridges generations, ensuring its mission endures in meaningful ways.

Embracing Technology and Social Issues for Youth Inclusion

Today's youth live in a digital age where technology shapes nearly every aspect of their lives. Engaging young congregants effectively requires integrating technology into worship, outreach, and social justice activities (Campbell & Tsuria, 2021). Digital platforms provide spaces where younger members can connect, share, and express their faith in ways that align with their digital-native experiences (Smith & Snell, 2009). Moreover, addressing social justice issues through digital means resonates strongly with young adults, as they are drawn to causes that promote equality and fairness. By using technology to amplify its message, the Black Church can bridge the gap between faith and modernity, creating an inclusive space that feels relevant and inspiring for the younger generation (Ransby, 2018).

Addressing Future Social and Cultural Challenges

Preparing for Advances in Technology and Cultural Shifts

The rapid pace of technological change presents both a challenge and an opportunity for the Black Church. To remain accessible, the Church must incorporate these tools into its practices, ensuring that it meets people where they are in today's digital landscape. Churches that embrace technological advancements, such as live-streamed services and online communities, will find it easier to reach diverse audiences and expand their influence beyond traditional boundaries (Ransby, 2018). Recognizing the cultural shifts that impact how people engage with faith will enable the Black Church to remain a relevant and vital institution.

Responding to Secularization and Changing Faith Trends

One of the most significant challenges facing the Black Church is the increasing secularization of society. As previously mentioned, many young people identify as "spiritual but not religious," seeking spiritual fulfillment outside traditional religious frameworks (Smith & Snell, 2009). To engage these individuals, the Church must provide meaningful spiritual experiences that do not rely on rigid structures but instead emphasize personal growth, communal support, and the pursuit of justice. Programs that address modern spiritual needs can make the Church more inclusive, offering a space for all who seek purpose and connection.

Embracing Innovation While Maintaining Foundational Values

For the Black Church, the future lies in balancing innovation with its core values. While adaptation is necessary to remain relevant, it should never come at the cost of compromising the principles that define the Church's mission (Campbell & Tsuria, 2021). Integrating innovative worship practices and community engagement methods with longstanding beliefs allows the Church to evolve without losing its identity. This balance fosters a sense of continuity, ensuring that as the Church meets new demands, it remains rooted in its purpose of providing spiritual refuge, empowerment, and justice for the Black community (Ransby, 2018). By embracing the future while honoring its past, the Black Church can secure a legacy that inspires generations to come.

4

Community and the Gathering of Ourselves Together

THE BLACK CHURCH HAS LONG BEEN THE SPIRITUAL AND communal heartbeat of Black communities, anchoring individuals in times of joy and crisis alike. Serving as a vital refuge, it offers not only spiritual guidance but also a haven for collective resilience and identity. Hebrews 10:25 (*New King James Version*, 1982) emphasizes the significance of gathering together, urging believers not to forsake the assembly—a call that resonates deeply within the Black Church. This call to gather is not merely about physical proximity; it reflects a broader mission of fostering solidarity, social identity, and empowerment. In a world of shifting social landscapes and technological advances, the Black Church's role in creating and sustaining a community has remained steady and adaptive.

Historically, the Black Church has served as a center for worship and fellowship, but its influence extends far beyond these functions. During the era of slavery, when the majority of communal spaces were inaccessible, the Church became an underground haven where enslaved individuals could find community and strength (Avent & Cashwell, 2015). It was here that people shared stories, sought solace, and cultivated resilience, setting the foundation for a powerful community identity. These gatherings—whether in secret or open—fostered an unbreakable bond among congregants, reinforcing the church's role as a center of unity and fortitude. The church served as a critical organizing ground for liberation efforts, with its role continuing through the Civil Rights Movement. Black churches provided spaces for strategic planning, transforming sermons and songs into powerful tools for mobilizing against injustice (Spencer, 2022). Through these gatherings, the Black Church not only built a communal identity but actively fueled the drive for justice and equality.

In contemporary times, Sunday worship remains central to the Black Church, bringing congregants together in a shared spiritual experience. These weekly gatherings create a sense of unity that strengthens the communal fabric as members join in singing, praying, and listening to sermons that address both personal and collective struggles. The collective experience of worship fosters a unity that speaks to the heart of the Black Church's mission, reinforcing bonds through shared faith and spiritual upliftment (Wilmore, 1998). However, the importance of gathering now transcends physical boundaries. The COVID-19 pandemic demonstrated the necessity of virtual gatherings, allowing churches to reach congregants who could not attend in person. While virtual services lack the sensory depth of in-person worship, they expand accessibility, bridging distances and circumstances that once separated members of the community.

Gathering in the Black Church also extends beyond worship, forming a foundation for social support and holistic well-being. Historically, the Black Church has been a place where members find emotional, financial, and spiritual assistance, creating an environment where every individual feels seen and valued. Through prayer meetings, community events, and Bible studies, the Black Church has cultivated a space where shared experiences and mutual support reinforce a sense of belonging. This communal identity not only offers solace but actively builds resilience, equipping congregants with the support they need to face challenges in their lives. Here, the Black Church functions as more than a religious institution; it is a community center where the spiritual meets the social in shared purpose and collective action.

In fostering a space that unites generations, the Black Church becomes a conduit for intergenerational knowledge and tradition. Elders share wisdom rooted in history and lived experience, while younger members bring fresh perspectives and innovation. This exchange is vital for preserving cultural identity and ensuring the continuity of the church's mission. As the Black Church adapts to an ever-evolving world, the wisdom passed down from generation to generation strengthens its resilience, allowing it to stand as a pillar of cultural and spiritual heritage (Smith & Snell, 2009). Through these intergenerational gatherings, the Church preserves its legacy, adapting its methods without sacrificing its core mission of communal support and spiritual guidance.

By embracing both physical and virtual spaces, the Black Church ensures that no member is left behind. Virtual platforms have enabled churches to extend their reach, connecting with those who have moved away or face physical limitations. While these digital gatherings cannot fully replicate the tangible warmth of in-person fellowship, they offer a crucial link for members who would otherwise be isolated, preserving the communal fabric during times of separation. Both forms of gathering will remain vital in upholding the Black Church's commitment to unity, resilience, and identity. Gathering—whether in sanctuaries, living rooms, or online spaces—continues to embody the Black Church's enduring dedication to its people, sustaining a community that thrives on solidarity and shared purpose.

Historical and Contemporary Role of Physical Gatherings in the Black Church

The Black Church and Civil Rights Activism

As discussed in previous chapters, during the Civil Rights Movement, Black churches became command centers for the pursuit of justice. Pastors and congregants transformed sacred spaces into hubs of planning and mobilization, weaving urgency for freedom, dignity, and equality into sermons, hymns, and prayers. For instance,

Rev. Fred Shuttlesworth organized direct action campaigns in Birmingham through Bethel Baptist Church, while Rev. William Holmes Borders championed economic uplift and civil rights at Wheat Street Baptist Church in Atlanta. Essayist William F. Spencer (2022) describes these churches as "free spaces" (p. 27)—crucial gathering spots where activists forged strategies and found the courage to push for systemic change. Theological scholars like Anthony B. Pinn (2002) have underscored the Church's dual impact, asserting that it not only offered moral direction but also served as a vital political engine, fueling grassroots action for equality.

The Civil Rights Movement left a lasting imprint on the Black Church, one that resonates to this day. Modern social movements, including Black Lives Matter, continue to rely on this legacy. Many congregations remain active in voter registration drives, hold awareness events, and speak out against systemic injustices. Professor Jeffrey S. Levin called the Black Church "the preserver and perpetuator of the black ethos" (J. Williams et al., 2019, p. 3), a social institution that lives up to its sacred mission by nurturing both hope and accountability. This ongoing relevance leads us to ask: How do we honor this heritage? In what ways does today's Church sustain its role as a sanctuary of social justice?

Even now, the Black Church serves as a powerful voice for change. The Church continually adapts to meet evolving societal needs, offering educational programs, social services, and opportunities for dialogue. Rooted in its enduring tradition of activism, the Church invites everyone to participate in shaping a more equitable future—one informed by the lessons of past struggles. In doing so, it challenges each of us to consider how we might embody its commitment to justice in our own lives and communities.

Sunday Worship Services as Community Foundation

Sunday service serves as the cornerstone of community existence within the Black Church. These weekly gatherings represent the fundamental principles of unity, resilience, and spiritual affirmation, transcending mere ritualistic regularity. Congregants unite to commemorate their common faith, strengthen one another in adversity, and derive strength from communal worship. Sunday services feature impactful experiences of singing, prayer, and preaching that evoke shared significance, strengthening communal ties (Spencer, 2022).

The energy of Sunday worship cultivates a distinctive, familial ambiance in which each person is both bolstered by and bolstering to people in their presence. This community assembly functions as a weekly reaffirmation of the Black Church's mission, uniting individuals in a profoundly spiritual manner. The communal experience of Sunday worship enables participants to contemplate the faith they practice, derive strength from each other, and reinforce their determination to confront life's adversities with fortitude and optimism.

Sunday worship transcends a mere weekly assembly; it represents the essence of communal existence in the Black Church, encapsulating perseverance, solidarity, and spiritual affirmation. These services are distinguished by a familial closeness when members provide mutual support and openly discuss their faith. The assembly features lively gospel music, impactful speeches, and communal prayer, strengthening the community's shared ideals and honoring individual dignity within a collective framework (Spencer, 2022). This weekly declaration of faith cultivates a profound sense of oneness, empowering congregations to confront life's problems with revitalized vigor.

The Role of Prayer Groups and Gospel Music in Community Action

Prayer groups and gospel music have emerged as significant motivators for community engagement within the Black Church. As Sandra L. Barnes (2005) explains, prayer groups provide spiritual support that extends to active community involvement. Through prayer, congregants find collective strength and a sense of responsibility to address societal needs, leading to actions that range from supporting local causes to participating in larger social movements (Barnes, 2005). Gospel music similarly resonates deeply within the Black Church, acting as a catalyst for community participation. Not simply an element of worship, gospel music reflects and reinforces the Church's commitment to social justice and unity, often prompting members to engage in outreach and activism as an extension of their faith (Barnes, 2005).

Hip-Hop as Worship: Expanding Church Culture and Accessibility

In recent years, hip-hop has found a place within some Black Church communities as a form of worship, reimagining religious expression for younger and more culturally diverse congregations. Hip Hop Church L.A., for example, incorporates hip-hop music and elements of rap in worship, aligning with the cultural experiences of urban youth and redefining the landscape of Black worship. Kurtis Blow, a pioneer in commercial rap, collaborated with Rev. Carol Scott to create a space where hip-hop could serve as a medium for faith. This unique approach resonates with attendees who might feel alienated by traditional church structures. By integrating hip-hop, the Black Church not only reaches a broader demographic but also affirms the worth of culturally relevant expressions of worship (Zanfagna, 2017).

In this hip-hop ministry, music is not just entertainment; it's a tool for worship and outreach, conveying messages of strength and divine empathy. As one participant expressed, "This is not entertainment; this is not a show. This is ministry" (Zanfagna, 2017, p. 3). For many who have experienced marginalization or urban struggles, hip-hop provides a language through which they can connect with the divine. The lyrics, rhythm, and energy of hip-hop worship create a dynamic, relatable space that honors their life experiences and invites them into a spiritual community.

The Transformative Power of Worship in a Diverse Church Community

As worship in the Black Church evolves, the integration of diverse elements like gospel, prayer, and hip-hop signifies a broader cultural embrace that transcends traditional boundaries. These elements of worship, whether through traditional gospel or modern hip-hop, not only enhance the Church's spiritual mission but also establish it as a responsive and inclusive institution. Through such adaptations, the Black Church continues to uplift its congregants and communities, affirming their value and agency in the face of societal challenges.

Preferences for Congregational Identity: The Role of Race and Worship Style

Race plays a unique role in shaping Black Americans' preferences for congregations, often influenced by the shared experiences of those within the community. When questioned about their reasons for attending their place of worship or how they would select a new one, even those who were part of historically Black Protestant denominations did not always highlight the racial makeup of their church as a primary factor (Mohamed et al., 2021). Instead, many are drawn to congregations based on the worship style, music, or preaching approach, which often reflects the broader cultural values and traditions that resonate within the Black community.

The Value of Predominantly Black Congregations

Historically, Black congregations have served as safe havens, offering protection from discrimination, providing familiar worship styles, and addressing the unique spiritual, social, and cultural needs of Black Americans. These congregations often reflect the communal values and collective resilience that have characterized the Black Church as a social institution. As one participant noted, "The Black Church that we know, based on the documentaries that I also [have] seen, was the gathering place for our strategizing and organizing" (Mohamed et al., 2021, p. 30). This historical role endures, with Black churches continuing to serve as safe spaces where members feel both spiritually and culturally connected.

Predominantly Black congregations also offer worship styles—such as gospel music, expressive preaching, and communal prayer—that resonate with the lived experiences of Black Americans. These worship elements not only enhance spiritual engagement but also reinforce cultural identity. In a society where systemic barriers persist, predominantly Black congregations provide a consistent and affirming environment that helps members navigate the challenges they face.

Challenges of Racial Integration in Other Congregations

Despite the preference for predominantly Black congregations, some Black Americans are open to worshiping in racially diverse settings. However, many encounter discomfort or even discrimination in these spaces, highlighting a need for greater inclusivity within religious environments. Participants described challenges in feeling truly accepted or represented in congregations that lacked a Black leadership presence. This underscores a recurring concern: the difficulty of finding a religious space where Black Americans can fully express their faith without the constraints or biases of racial discrimination.

For instance, one participant shared, "My church is not a segregating church. It's segregated, but not segregating. It would welcome White members" (Mohamed et al., 2021, p. 32). This distinction underscores an openness to inclusivity in many Black congregations, even as they maintain a predominantly Black identity. As another participant put it, "Church has no color to me, because anyone's invited to come there, whether they're Black, whether they're Chinese, Spanish or whatever" (p. 31).

The Black Church as a Common Language

Across generations, the Black Church has functioned as a unifying force, shaping how individuals view themselves, connect with one another, and resist systemic injustices. It has long served as a sort of "common language"—a channel through which African Americans share core values, history, and collective purpose. Sociologist Pattillo-McCoy (1998) identifies Black church culture as a "common language that motivates social action" woven into prayer, call-and-response, and Christian symbolism (p. 3). These practices transcend traditional religious boundaries, infusing everyday gatherings with a consistent cultural rhythm that roots the Black community in a shared identity.

One of the clearest examples of this shared language is the practice of call-and-response. In these moments, the preacher's words resonate through the congregation, prompting a unified reply that turns the sermon into a communal declaration of faith and perseverance. This dynamic echoes African oral traditions, working as a "cultural tool kit" that aligns people around common beliefs and ideals (Pattillo-McCoy, 1998, p. 15). As voices blend together, the Church becomes more than just a building; it becomes an ark, carrying the community's collective spirit, memories, and hopes.

This communal language also shines through in the shared rituals of prayer and song, which extend well beyond Sunday services. In times of celebration or sorrow, people often turn to familiar prayer circles, gospel music, and scriptural references, using them to connect with one another and find comfort. These actions transcend individual faith practices, uniting community members under a collective banner of resilience and support. Through such moments, the Black Church's cultural expressions become acts of solidarity, woven into the very essence of African American identity.

The Church as a Community Anchor

As previously discussed, the Black Church has always served as more than a house of worship. Over the decades, it has evolved into a multifaceted support system, offering spiritual grounding, social advocacy, and critical resources that promote resilience and empowerment. Historian Evelyn Brooks Higginbotham (1993) highlights how the Church fulfills a dual role as spiritual haven and civic engine, blending faith practices with tangible initiatives that uplift its congregants. This balance speaks to the Black Church's ongoing significance as a stabilizing force, especially in the face of ever-changing social landscapes.

During the Civil Rights Movement, the Black Church emerged as a vital hub for mobilization. Its sanctuaries served as strategic meeting places for organizing voter registration, planning rallies, and shaping the broader movement for equality. Leaders like Rev. Dr. Martin Luther King Jr. and Rev. Fred Shuttlesworth harnessed the power of these sacred spaces not only to inspire hope but also to unite communities around a common goal. By serving as both refuge and launchpad for social change, the Black Church reinforced its essential role as a driver of progress.

Today, the Black Church continues that legacy by tackling modern challenges, from economic inequality and educational gaps to health crises. Many congregations offer financial literacy programs, job training, and scholarships, helping members build a sustainable future. These efforts reaffirm the Church's commitment to the well-being of its community—a covenant that extends beyond the safe haven and into every aspect of daily life.

Furthermore, the Black Church remains a powerful advocate for systemic reform, whether it's challenging mass incarceration, pushing for police accountability, or strengthening voting rights. By partnering with grassroots organizations and elevating crucial conversations, churches demonstrate that faith and justice are deeply intertwined. This work reflects the Church's role as a bridge between the sacred and the social—a place where spiritual principles animate real-world calls for equity and opportunity.

The Black Church as a Cultural Strategy for Social Action

In challenging times, the Black Church acts as a powerful force for bringing people together and driving change. Church leaders often draw on biblical stories—like the Exodus, symbolizing freedom from oppression, or Job's trials, highlighting faith in suffering—to show how ancient struggles connect to the injustices African Americans face today (Higginbotham, 1993). By focusing on themes of liberation, justice, and hope, these sermons give congregants both a moral compass and a sense of unity.

The Church also strategically uses Christian symbols and language—such as the Cross, the Ark of the Covenant, and the concept of the Promised Land—to empower members. These images go beyond their religious origins, speaking directly to the journey from enslavement to freedom and from exclusion to equality (Wilmore, 1983). As Glaude (2020) points out, blending faith and cultural identity transforms worship spaces into places of resilience and activism, where history and spiritual commitment come together.

Through these cultural tools, the Black Church unites people around both faith and action. Communal events and rituals allow members to share personal stories, celebrate accomplishments, and confront challenges together. By keeping symbols of resilience alive in everyday life, the Church encourages members to tackle modern issues like economic inequality, racial injustice, and voter suppression. When sacred symbols are reimagined as practical resources, the Black Church continues to kindle collective hope and determination, guiding its community toward a more equitable future.

The Black Church as an Intergenerational Ark: Bridging Legacy and Innovation

The Black Church thrives as a meeting place where the wisdom of elders meets the energy and creativity of youth. More than a place of worship, it's a space where generations come together to share knowledge, stories, and dreams. This unique role makes the Church a bridge between the past and the future, blending the strength of its traditions with fresh ideas to face today's challenges.

Elders bring lessons from the past, shaped by struggles like slavery, segregation, and the Civil Rights Movement. Their stories and songs are reminders of perseverance and a roadmap for navigating injustice. At the same time, younger members bring new perspectives and approaches to tackle issues like mental health, economic inequality, and climate justice. These exchanges aren't just meaningful—they're the heartbeat of the Black Church, ensuring its legacy stays relevant while embracing the future.

Keeping Traditions Alive While Embracing Change

Like the Ark of the Covenant symbolized continuity for the Israelites, the Black Church connects the community's spiritual past to its evolving future. Traditions like gospel music, for example, continue to inspire while adapting to modern influences. Sermons, too, are evolving, addressing today's realities—whether it's financial empowerment, mental health, or systemic racism—while staying rooted in biblical truths. This balance keeps the Church at the center of the community, offering something timeless yet always relevant.

By holding onto its roots while adapting to the times, the Black Church remains a safe place where people find hope, purpose, and a sense of belonging. It's the Church's ability to change without losing its identity that keeps it strong.

Building Bridges Between Generations

To stay vibrant, the Black Church needs to create more opportunities for generations to connect. Mentorship programs, shared leadership roles, and creative worship styles can bring elders and young leaders closer together. These efforts deepen the bonds that make the Church a community, ensuring it speaks to every generation.

Role of Elders and Generational Wisdom

The elders in the Black Church hold a revered position as the custodians of wisdom and lived experience, essential for maintaining the Church's legacy. As spiritual mentors, they guide congregants through spiritual, social, and sometimes even health-related challenges. These elders often embody the Church's rich history, having lived through transformative eras such as the Civil Rights Movement, and their stories anchor the congregation to a legacy of faith.

The wisdom shared by these elders goes beyond doctrine; it encompasses life lessons and cultural values that nurture a sense of identity and pride among younger generations. For many, the Black Church is not just a place of worship but a social institution where generational knowledge is preserved through the narratives and teachings of elders. This process is akin to passing down a treasured family heirloom, with each story, lesson, and piece of advice contributing to the foundation of the community's collective memory and identity. Through regular gatherings, elders impart this wisdom, reinforcing the Black Church as a vital community structure.

This intergenerational exchange also offers younger members a sense of continuity, connecting them to the struggles and triumphs of those who came before. As elders share their insights, younger congregants are reminded of their community's resilience and are inspired to carry forward these values. The Black Church, in this way, serves as a bridge linking past, present, and future generations.

Youth Engagement and Preserving Tradition

Engaging youth in the life of the Church is essential for preserving its cultural and spiritual legacy. In recent years, Black churches have recognized the importance of developing programs that are culturally relevant and resonate with the younger generation's unique experiences and challenges. By tailoring activities to address contemporary issues within a spiritual context, churches foster a sense of belonging and purpose among their younger members.

Youth programs in the Black Church often focus on more than spiritual growth—they address physical and social well-being as well. Activities such as community service, health initiatives, and mentorship programs not only enrich the lives of young congregants but also connect them to their cultural heritage. For example, health programs led by the Church promote well-being while tying in values of faith and community care, reinforcing the idea that spiritual and physical wellness are intertwined aspects of a fulfilling life. Through these programs, youth gain a deeper understanding of their heritage and are reminded that their role in the Church is essential.

Involving young people in church activities also offers them a sense of responsibility and agency within the community. The inclusion of youth in church governance, events, and service roles creates a dynamic where they contribute fresh ideas and energy, helping to keep the Church relevant in a rapidly changing world. This engagement fosters a generational continuity that ensures the values and traditions of the Black Church endure.

The Black Church's approach to youth engagement goes beyond typical religious education; it actively encourages young members to develop a meaningful connection with their cultural and spiritual heritage. By empowering them to take part in church life, the Church instills in them a sense of belonging and purpose that they can carry into the future. This intentional investment in youth not only strengthens the Church's present community but also secures its mission for generations to come. Through these intergenerational relationships, the Black Church continues to be a cornerstone for the African American community, binding past, present, and future together in a shared journey of faith and resilience.

5

Preserving Black Culture Through Sacred Traditions

THE BLACK CHURCH IS THE LONG-SERVING GUARDIAN of Black cultural identity, acting as a steadfast steward in preserving essential elements of African American heritage that might otherwise dissipate within broader societal currents. This sacred space is where the legacies of resilience, resistance, and faith intersect, enabling Black individuals to celebrate, nurture, and pass down the traditions that have shaped their history. Sacred traditions such as gospel music, call-and-response preaching, and communal rituals remain central to this mission. These sacred traditions create touchstones that bind generations in shared identity and purpose, underscore the Church's role in fostering cultural continuity, and provide refuge during times of struggle.

Gospel Music: A Pillar of Black Cultural Identity

Origins of Gospel Music and Its African Roots

Gospel music stands as one of the most profound contributions of the Black Church, embodying both spiritual depth and cultural resilience. Rooted in African rhythms and evolving from the Negro spirituals of enslaved communities, gospel music has transformed over the decades, carrying forward the messages of faith and endurance that defined its early beginnings. Songs like "The Lord Will Make a Way Somehow" and "Wait on Jesus" capture this legacy, acting as musical embodiments of survival and spiritual fortitude. Today, gospel music continues to help African Americans navigate the hardships of life with faith and hope.

The Rich Symbolism of Gospel Music

Gospel music stands as one of the Black Church's deepest cultural legacies. This genre is not simply music; it is an expression of the struggles and the victories of Black people across generations. Rooted in the rich soil of African traditions, gospel music evolved from the sorrow-filled spirituals of enslaved Africans, bearing witness to the hardships endured and the hope that sustained them.

The heartbeat of gospel is felt in its rhythm and lyrics, which carry the weight of history while inspiring listeners to persevere. For many Black Americans, gospel is an invitation to commune with ancestors and express a faith grounded in resilience. This music transcends entertainment—it is a sacred expression, a way of communicating our shared experiences and drawing us closer to each other and our heritage. Through gospel, we find our spiritual bearings, allowing us to anchor our identity in something deeply meaningful.

Influence of African Traditions in Rhythm, Melody, and Storytelling

Gospel music's roots trace back to African rhythms and melodic structures, carried to the Americas during the transatlantic slave trade. These musical traditions, with their characteristic beats, chants, and call-and-response patterns, found new life in the form of Negro spirituals.

These early songs were more than mere expressions of faith; they were cultural survival tools, embedding coded messages and communal resilience.

In *Somebody's Calling My Name*, Wyatt Tee Walker emphasizes the Black Church's role as the primary preserver of African heritage in the United States, with worship practices rooted in African traditions that have transcended centuries and slavery. Walker describes the Black Church as "the American fruit of an African root," where spiritual practices, especially music, retain African influences and cultural values (Walker, 1979, p. 22). This African-rooted worship style, evident in gospel music and congregational participation, maintains a living connection to ancestral practices, reinforcing cultural identity within the Black community.

Walker explores how Black sacred music—whether through field songs, gospel, or congregational hymns—serves as an effective vehicle for cultural preservation and continuity. In this context, music within the Black Church is more than an element of worship; it is a cultural expression that fosters collective memory and identity, shaping how congregants experience and express their faith. By drawing on traditional African musical elements like rhythm, call-and-response, and communal participation, the Black Church retains and celebrates its cultural heritage. Walker observes that this authentic musical style allows for a worship experience "undeniably emotion-evoking," establishing the church as a unique cultural space where African values of community, resilience, and spiritual strength continue to flourish (Walker, 1979, p. 26).

Through African-rooted music, the Black Church not only preserves a critical link to African heritage but also empowers its community with a shared identity. This tradition of worship distinguishes Black congregations from Euro-American religious practices, where restraint often replaces the exuberant expression native to African-derived cultures. In prioritizing cultural continuity, the Black Church solidifies its role as a vital guardian of African American identity, ensuring that worship remains a space for cultural preservation and spiritual empowerment.

Development of Gospel Music Through Spirituals and Hymns

Hymns and Spirituals resonated deeply with African Americans. These songs provided spiritual comfort in times of despair offering hope and deliverance throughout the Black community. The songs themselves became cultural texts, with each note and lyric narrating the journey of Black communities navigating oppression and finding solace in faith.

Evolution and Impact of Gospel Music Through the Civil Rights Movement

Gospel as a Unifying and Empowering Force During the Civil Rights Era

During the Civil Rights Movement, gospel music became a powerful symbol of unity and resistance. Songs like "We Shall Overcome" transformed from worship anthems into battle cries, galvanizing protesters and fostering solidarity among activists. Mahalia Jackson, an icon of gospel music, sang with a purpose beyond performance; her powerful contralto helped to spread a message of unity and energize people in their pursuit of justice. Gospel music was a bridge between faith and activism, reinforcing the idea that the pursuit of civil rights was a holy calling.

Influence of Iconic Gospel Figures in Popularizing Gospel Music

Figures like Mahalia Jackson, who collaborated closely with Dr. Martin Luther King Jr., helped elevate gospel music from church pews to national stages, influencing the broader culture. Jackson's performances at rallies and marches infused the movement with spiritual fervor, reminding participants that their struggle was grounded in a shared faith. Her contributions popularized gospel music, bringing its messages of hope and liberation to diverse audiences. Through songs like "We Shall Overcome," gospel music transformed from an art form into a powerful vehicle for social change, affirming the Church's role as a cultural and spiritual refuge.

Gospel's Reach Beyond the Black Church

Influence on Mainstream Music and Culture

Gospel's influence extends beyond the walls of the Black Church, shaping genres like blues, jazz, and rock, and embedding African American cultural elements in mainstream American music. This genre's unique blend of spirituality and resilience has made it a foundational element of the nation's musical landscape, shaping a collective African American identity that has influenced artists across racial and cultural lines.

Role of Gospel in Connecting Diverse Audiences to Black Cultural Heritage

Today, gospel music is celebrated globally, connecting diverse audiences with the rich cultural heritage of the Black Church. Its themes of redemption, hope, and endurance resonate universally, making gospel choirs and songs beloved across continents. Through gospel, the Black Church has achieved an enduring impact, preserving cultural traditions while bridging cultural divides.

Call-and-Response Preaching

A Sacred Dialogue

The tradition of call-and-response preaching represents another vital cultural thread within the Black Church. This dynamic and interactive form of worship is deeply rooted in African oral traditions, fostering a sense of community and shared spiritual experience. In this sacred dialogue, the preacher's call invites the congregation's response, creating a rhythm of affirmation and connection. This participatory style is not merely a performance but an invocation of unity, allowing worshippers to reaffirm their faith and feel an active part of the congregation's spiritual journey.

A Tradition of Empowerment and Adaptation

Call-and-response preaching is more than a hallmark of the Black Church; it is a deeply emotional and cultural exchange that brings sermons to life. Rooted in African oral traditions, call-and-response preaching carries the rhythm of resilience and joy, allowing every voice in the room to feel heard, seen, and connected.

The emotional impact of call-and-response preaching is profound. An emphatic "Amen" or "Hallelujah" reverberates through the congregation to unite individuals in a shared moment of spiritual awakening. For generations, this tradition has served as a source of empowerment, affirming the dignity and strength of a community that has often faced systemic oppression. It reminds participants that they are not just passive listeners but active participants in their own faith journey.

In recent years, this sacred tradition has adapted to modern worship practices. As virtual services have become more common, especially during the COVID-19 pandemic, digital platforms have given new life to call-and-response preaching. Chat boxes, emojis, and live reactions have become the congregation's virtual "Amens," preserving the participatory essence of worship even in digital spaces. Preachers, too, have embraced this shift, finding ways to engage their online audiences with the same energy and inclusivity that define in-person services.

Call-and-response preaching remains a testament to the adaptability and vibrancy of the Black Church. It bridges the past and present, carrying forward a tradition that empowers the spirit while embracing new forms of connection. Whether in a packed church or through a digital screen, this sacred dialogue continues to inspire and unite, ensuring that every voice finds a place in the story of faith.

African Origins and Cultural Significance of Call-and-Response

Influence of African Oral Traditions in Worship

Call-and-response in the Black Church draws directly from African oral traditions where communal participation is fundamental. In African cultures, verbal affirmations and rhythmic responses were central to communal events and ceremonies, creating a living dialogue that united individuals in shared identity and purpose. This tradition's presence in Black churches highlights a cultural legacy that has endured through generations, symbolizing both faith and heritage. This interactive worship style transforms services into "events of shared affirmation and solidarity" that link African Americans with the storytelling practices of their ancestors.

Embedding Heritage in Worship

In call-and-response, the congregation is more than an audience; they are active participants, engaging in a form of worship that allows each individual's voice to contribute to the sacred dialogue. This act of participation, known as the "Amen corner," gives congregants the opportunity to affirm their beliefs aloud, cultivating a powerful unity that intertwines spirituality and cultural identity. The cultural significance of this practice lies in its ability to make worship a shared journey, resonating with members who feel seen, heard, and spiritually renewed through their involvement.

Call-and-Response as a Community-Building Practice

Transforming Worship Into a Collective Event

Call-and-response is not only a form of engagement but also a bridge that links individuals within the congregation, fostering a communal experience that merges the spiritual and social lives of worshippers. By affirming the words of the preacher, the congregation transforms from passive listeners to active participants, reinforcing a sense of unity and shared values. This dynamic interaction is an integral part of the sermon for both pastors and their congregants.

Fostering Belonging and Collective Identity

Through call-and-response, worship becomes an immersive experience that binds individuals through their shared faith and identity. This practice enables congregants to feel a deep connection not only with each other but also with the broader history and traditions of the Black Church. This tradition cultivates a unique space where each person's voice is valued, and the congregation's collective power becomes a testament to their resilience and unity.

Impact on Collective Identity and Worship Experience

In *Spirits That Dwell in Deep Woods II: The Prayer and Praise Hymns of the Black Religious Experience*, Wyatt Tee Walker delves into the unique value of prayer as a cornerstone of worship in the Black Church. Through his exploration of hymns like "Jesus on the Mainline," Walker illustrates how prayer within the Black worship tradition transcends a personal connection with God, becoming a communal act of solidarity and resilience. This hymn, he explains, is not just a song but a vehicle for theological truth, portraying Jesus as "only a phone call away" (Walker, 1988, p. 45). This imagery reinforces the sense of accessibility to the divine, a belief deeply embedded in the Black Church's worship culture. In Black congregational life, prayer and worship are marked by a strong conviction in God's immediacy and responsiveness, a faith in divine companionship that is foundational to the Black Church experience.

Walker's analysis of prayer reveals a powerful aspect of worship in the Black Church: the communal reassurance that, through worship, congregants are not isolated in their struggles (1988). Prayer, as Walker suggests, is a force of unity, binding individuals together as they vocalize shared hopes, needs, and praise. This understanding reflects a broader characteristic of Black worship, where collective prayer becomes a declaration of faith and mutual support, affirming the belief that each member's burdens are shared by the community and supported by God. By depicting Jesus as near and available, hymns like "Jesus on the Mainline" function as affirmations of God's presence within and among worshippers, reinforcing the Church's role as both a spiritual refuge and a source of strength.

Moreover, Walker (1988) emphasizes that this tradition of prayer and hymn-singing goes beyond personal devotion; it is deeply intertwined with cultural heritage and resilience. For the Black Church, hymns are a communal language of faith and hope, shared across generations to sustain spiritual life amidst hardship. Worship, then, becomes a living, communal expression of reliance on God, grounded in the belief that God answers prayers. Walker's observations affirm that worship in the Black Church is an act of collective empowerment, where prayer not only connects believers with the divine but also strengthens their unity and perseverance as a community.

Reinforcing Cultural Heritage Through Sacred Dialogue

For many Black congregants, call-and-response is more than an expression of faith; it is a vital connection to their cultural heritage. It acts as a bridge that connects their present worship with the practices of their ancestors, allowing them to feel both spiritually grounded and culturally affirmed. By engaging in this tradition, congregants not only affirm their beliefs but also participate in a ritual that honors their community's heritage.

Ritualized Expressions of Faith: Symbols of Commitment and Continuity

The Black Church has long embraced ritualized expressions of faith as profound moments of spiritual connection, cultural continuity, and communal unity. Practices like altar calls, communion services, and baptism are more than religious ceremonies; they are sacred milestones that reaffirm an individual's commitment to faith while strengthening the collective bonds of the congregation.

Altar calls provide opportunities for personal transformation within a communal setting. When individuals step forward to pray, recommit their lives, or seek guidance, the congregation surrounds them with support, embodying the Black Church's role as a nurturing, restorative space. Similarly, baptism serves as a symbol of rebirth and belonging, connecting participants to the broader Christian tradition while reinforcing their identity within the Black community. Communion, with its deep ties to remembrance and unity, brings congregants together to honor both their spiritual lineage and their collective mission.

These rituals carry a unique cultural resonance within the Black Church, much like the Ark of the Covenant carried sacred meaning for the Israelites. Just as the Ark symbolized God's covenant with His people, these practices affirm the Black Church's covenantal role in preserving faith, identity, and solidarity. They serve as tangible reminders of God's presence and promises, offering renewal in moments of challenge and celebration alike.

In a modern context, these rituals remain as relevant as ever, providing stability and meaning in an ever-changing world. Their enduring power lies in their ability to bridge past and present, connecting congregants to their ancestors' faith while equipping them to navigate the complexities of contemporary life. By fostering a shared sense of purpose and belonging, ritualized expressions of faith ensure the Black Church continues to thrive as a source of spiritual and cultural strength.

Altar Calls: Moments of Commitment and Renewal

Public Declaration and Community Support

An altar call is a powerful invitation for personal reflection, commitment, and spiritual renewal. This practice invites congregants to come forward, symbolizing a public declaration of faith and a renewed commitment to their spiritual journey. Here, congregants are encouraged to surrender their concerns, renew their faith, and receive prayers from the church community, which acts as both a witness and a source of support. This tradition underscores the collective nature of the Black Church, where personal faith journeys are shared and celebrated within the larger community.

Bridging Personal Conviction With Public Accountability

In the Black Church, altar calls embody both personal conviction and public accountability, transforming individual faith decisions into communal events. As congregants step forward, their journey becomes intertwined with that of the broader church body, where every declaration of faith is seen as an act of collective strength and unity. This transformative ritual reinforces the interconnectedness of personal spirituality and community responsibility. Altar calls thus stand as moments of both personal renewal and public accountability, ensuring that each commitment is strengthened within a community that witnesses and supports these expressions of faith.

Communion Service: Unity Through Sacrament

Remembering Sacrifice and Collective Values

The communion service, or the "breaking of bread," is a sacred tradition within the Black Church that invites congregants to remember the humility, sacrifice, and love exemplified by Jesus. Through this sacrament, the congregation not only reflects on Jesus's sacrifice but also recommits to the values of service, unity, and love. This act of remembrance unites worshippers in a profound acknowledgment of the shared beliefs that sustain their community.

Fostering Historical and Spiritual Continuity

Within Black churches, communion is not only a spiritual ritual but also a moment of deep historical connection. This shared experience strengthens bonds within the congregation and with the generations who came before and whose faith and resilience remain a source of inspiration.

Baptism: Rebirth and Dedication to Faith

A Symbol of Rebirth and Lifelong Commitment

Baptism within the Black Church holds profound significance as both a rite of passage and a public commitment to live according to the teachings of Christ. It symbolizes a spiritual rebirth, marking a transition into a life of faith and community belonging. This ritual affirms the individual's commitment to Christian values and the support they will receive from the church as they embark on this journey.

Integrating Individual and Community Support

In the context of the Black Church, baptism is both an individual and a communal declaration. As each new believer emerges from the water, they are welcomed into a supportive community that commits to nurturing and guiding them. This communal aspect of baptism embodies the Church's dedication to collective spiritual growth and accountability, ensuring that the journey of faith is not undertaken alone. Baptism in the Black Church context often involves community support because congregants commit to nurturing and guiding the baptized individual in their faith journey. This shared responsibility underscores the Church's role as a guardian of both individual and collective faith, fostering a sense of belonging and shared commitment among all members.

Storytelling and Oral History: Preserving the Past, Inspiring the Future

The Black Church has always been a guardian of collective memory, using storytelling and oral history to preserve the struggles, triumphs, and faith of the African American community. Through sermons, testimonies, prayers, and communal narratives, the Church creates a sacred space where the past meets the present, offering lessons of endurance and inspiration for the future. This tradition is not simply about recounting history; it is about weaving the lived experiences of generations into a tapestry that affirms identity and purpose.

In the testimonies of elders, the prayers of ancestors, and the hymns that echo through sanctuaries, the Black Church safeguards cultural memory. These stories are not relics of the past; they are living, breathing reminders of the community's enduring spirit. They capture the essence of survival against oppression, turning pain into purpose and hardship into hope. By preserving these narratives, the Church equips younger generations with the knowledge of where they come from and the courage to envision where they can go.

Unlike static artifacts, the oral traditions of the Black Church are dynamic and adaptive, shifting to reflect the needs and challenges of the present moment. Stories of the past are used to frame contemporary struggles, connecting the trials of yesterday with the victories of today. In this way, storytelling becomes both a cultural anchor and a prophetic tool, inspiring congregants to carry forward the legacy of strength, justice, and faith.

Rather than focusing solely on what has been, the act of storytelling in the Black Church shapes what can be. These shared narratives do more than preserve heritage; they ignite action, calling each member to become part of a larger story, one that continually bends toward liberation, hope, and the power of faith. By honoring the stories of the past while envisioning a brighter future, the Black Church ensures its legacy remains vibrant, purposeful, and deeply rooted in the lives of its people.

6

Hearing the
Prophetic Voices

PROPHETIC LEADERSHIP HAS LONG DEFINED THE BLACK Church. From Nat Turner and Dr. Martin Luther King Jr. to contemporary voices like Rev. Al Sharpton, the Church has consistently produced leaders who speak truth to power, champion justice, and spark social change. This tradition is grounded in the belief that the Church must serve as both a voice for the voiceless and an advocate for the oppressed (K. Taylor, 2016). In this chapter, we examine the Church's prophetic role and the urgent need to amplify new voices in today's struggles for racial and economic justice.

At its core, the prophetic tradition of the Black Church is marked by the courage to confront injustice and disrupt the status quo. Nat Turner's rebellion, though often debated, represented an early assertion of the right to freedom and human dignity in the face of brutal oppression (Wilmore, 1998). Later, Dr. Martin

Luther King Jr. embodied this prophetic call through his leadership in the Civil Rights Movement. From the pulpit, he demanded an end to segregation, discrimination, and inequality. His vision of a "beloved community" was deeply rooted in faith and driven by the transforming power of love and justice (Lincoln & Mamiya, 1990).

In the present day, Rev. Sharpton continues this legacy through his work with NAN, tackling issues such as voter suppression, economic injustice, and unequal access to healthcare. His leadership affirms the Church's enduring role as an advocate for the most vulnerable in society (K. Taylor, 2016). Today's prophetic voices, however, are not limited to clergy. They include activists, organizers, and everyday individuals who boldly challenge oppression and call us to build a more just and equitable world.

This tradition is also visible in the Black Church's support of contemporary movements like Black Lives Matter. In response to police brutality and systemic racism, many churches and faith leaders have provided platforms for activists and created spaces for organizing, protest, and healing. In doing so, the Church continues its legacy of prophetic witness and remains a moral compass for the community.

As we face ongoing crises—racism, economic inequality, and mass incarceration—the need for prophetic leadership has never been greater. The Black Church must continue to be a platform for courageous voices, offering support and space to speak truth to power and inspire real change (Lincoln & Mamiya, 1990). By doing so, we honor the legacy of those who came before us and ensure that the prophetic spirit remains alive.

context, issues such as economic inequality and healthcare disparities are urgent concerns that the Church must confront. For example, as a response to economic disparity, Black churches have increasingly become involved in advocating for economic justice, supporting initiatives that provide job training, financial literacy, and resources to marginalized communities (Wilkes, 2024). Additionally, the Black Church has taken a stand on healthcare access, recognizing it as a matter of justice and equity. By focusing on these issues, the Church reinforces its prophetic identity, ensuring that its message of liberation remains relevant and impactful in the present day.

The Black Church as a Moral Compass

For centuries, the Church has not only addressed the spiritual concerns of Black communities but also served as a prominent critic of society's systemic injustices and pervasive inequities. The Black Church has always given and continues to give guidance and comfort from its pulpits. However, its role extends far beyond simply offering "come to Jesus" moments or serving as a "chill-out center" in times of community distress. The Black Church is a moral beacon, not shy about addressing political and social issues (Spencer, 2022), and it is also a cultural compass that thousands of community residents look to for leadership.

The Black Church has long been a space where one can engage in moral discourse that many—especially in the predominantly White Christian sphere—might consider quite problematic. Yet it does this without rendering the voices of others—especially those from non-Christian backgrounds—anything less than valuable. In fact, during the Civil Rights Movement, Black churches across the country (not just in the South) opened their doors to an astonishing array of figures—both spiritual and secular—who were believed to be helping along the way toward justice. Malcolm X, Minister Louis Farrakhan, and Coretta Scott King are just a few of the not-so-comfortable-for-some Christians figures who have addressed (and, in the case of Scott King, effectively pastored) Black church congregations.

This is a complicated, layered, and thick understanding of justice, which has emerged from the Church's profound moral teaching. Today, we might describe liberation theology as articulating "thin" and "thick" versions of justice. Both concern themselves with a broad array of social issues. Some practitioners engage in next-to-invisible acts of daily resistance. Others—indeed, many others, if recent history is any guide—act much more visibly and passionately. For those with a "thick" version of liberation theology, moving toward moral justice requires civil disobedience. Both pathways—the visible and the next-to-invisible—clearly lead to a social justice mission.

Educational and Economic Advocacy

The Black Church has made advocacy for justice on more than just a spiritual level its mission. It is working with other organizations to tackle the tough twin issues of educational and economic inequality that still plague a significant portion of our society. In doing so, it is redirecting its community's attention to whatever resources might be available to them and to pathways that might lead them to better conditions both socially and economically. The Black Church, in many communities, serves as a close-to-home authority in this work.

The Church demonstrates its dedication to education through various efforts, including tutoring programs and mentorship for kids, aimed at addressing the educational deficiencies in certain neighborhoods across the nation. The Church engages with these areas through a populist agenda that offers not only education but also the prospect of "transformative hope," which can facilitate genuine change, supported by the faith that many individuals in these communities uphold.

The Black Church has always advocated for a distinct set of policies aimed at attaining economic justice. Wilkes (2024) asserts that the primary objective of the Black Church has been economic empowerment, achieved not merely through charitable contributions but also by invoking the righteous wrath described by Martin Luther King Jr. as the powers that be. Focusing our academic inquiry on the fundamental mission of the Black Church and its enduring pursuit of economic justice enhances our comprehension of our own "poor suits."

The impact and prophetic legacy of the Black Church reach well beyond the confines of the United States. It resonates globally and acts as an impetus for marginalized populations striving for social justice. Communities in Africa, Latin America, and the Caribbean resonate with the words of the Black Church and serve as prominent locations where its influence illuminates as a symbol of hope. The global influence of the Black Church extends beyond the United States and is a driving force behind social justice movements worldwide.

Moreover, the Church demonstrates its global commitment to human rights and equality through collaborations with international justice initiatives. Justice must move beyond protest to shape the institutions that guide daily life. It should influence workplaces, schools, corporations, health systems, and more to bring lasting change to how society practices equality and pursues genuine diversity. The Black Church embodies this charge, insisting that faith be active in every sphere where injustice lingers and that moral clarity must never be confined within sacred walls. By joining forces with global movements, the Black Church makes what it stands for undeniably clear and aligns itself with rhetoric that no one with a shred of humanity would dare to contradict. When it talks about these values, we can be sure it's referring to an agenda as pertinent in Johannesburg, London, or Sydney as it is in Nashville, Montgomery, or Memphis. And the potent global actors—like the United Nations—also say these same potent words.

The prophetic Black Church is charged with developing and implementing a digital ministry if it is to keep pace and lend prophetic voice to a rapidly changing society. There is no choice but to engage the digital universe if there is to be any hope of reaching a wider—and especially a younger—audience. But entry into this promised land is not without its stumbling blocks. First among these is the digital divide, which encompasses both the Church and the community across which it is a "digital church." The next digital challenge—and it is a huge one—is that the digital presence of the Black Church is not and cannot be as good as its real-world presence when it comes to audience engagement. Finally, how can the Black Church engage in this promised land without first confronting the question of integrity and authenticity that is bound up with the very presence of the Church in a digital environment?

The Black Church has a pivotal task ahead: to reinvigorate itself in a society that's becoming more secular and, in the process, not to alienate those who are weaning themselves from conventional forms of religion. But it's not enough merely to coexist in this still-unfolding cultural transformation. The Black Church must also find ways to stay connected to a stunningly diverse generational membership that's not shy about its considerable differences.

The Black Church's innovation hinges on its faithfulness to the prophetic mission, and the new way of being a church calls for something more than the old media. New digital platforms, particularly the Internet, are part of the reframing. A distraction? No, for some figures of the Black Church, they are a means to an end. Collectively, these insights shine a light on the resilience and adaptability of the Black Church as it navigates an ever-mutating social landscape, sturdy as ever in upholding its time-honored role as a community moral compass.

Scandals and Trust Issues:
A Crisis of Faith in Church Leadership

In recent years, scandals within various religious institutions have taken a significant toll on the public's trust in church leaders, affecting the traditional role of churches as moral guides within their communities. As one commentator put it,

> When you look at what happened in the Catholic Church with the scandal with the priests, and some of the things that have happened recently— not just with African American pastors, but with megachurch pastors asking their congregants to buy a $55 million jet—these are the kinds of things that undermine people's faith in the church. (Mohamed, et al., 2021, p. 144.)

The erosion of trust is palpable. There was a time when church leaders held a place of unchallenged authority in the hearts of the people, serving as figures of reverence and respect. However, as another member noted, "It's nothing like it was. Pastors were highly reverent, highly respected, but with all the various scandals and moral lapses, the image, the respect, the role—it's just not the same" (Mohamed et al., 2021, p. 144). These sentiments highlight the significant shift in how religious leadership is perceived today, underscoring a disconnect that extends across denominations and communities.

This change isn't just about a few high-profile cases; it reflects a broader trend in how authority figures are viewed in a society increasingly skeptical of institutions. Once seen as the moral compass, the church now faces an uphill battle to restore its place as a trusted institution. This struggle is not unique to the Black Church, yet the impact is profound in communities where church leaders traditionally held the dual role of spiritual leader and community advocate.

Reflecting on these sentiments, it's clear that rebuilding trust will require more than words; it will take action, transparency, and a recommitment to the principles that first established the Church as a refuge and a moral foundation for many. Only then can church leaders hope to restore the integrity and trust that has been, for too long, eroded by a series of painful public scandals.

The Prophetic Tradition in the Black Church and Its Modern Manifestations

The prophetic tradition of the Black Church shines powerfully in its engagement with today's social movements, particularly Black Lives Matter, a movement ignited in response to police brutality and systemic racism, exemplifies this prophetic mission and has become an extension of the Black Church's legacy of social justice. Black churches and faith leaders across the nation have supported and amplified Black Lives Matter's demands for accountability, bringing the weight of their collective moral authority to bear against persistent racial violence and inequity. By offering spaces for activists to gather, pray, and strategize, the Black Church continues to serve as a vital force for transformation, reinforcing its commitment to justice and moral accountability.

Nurturing and Amplifying New Prophetic Voices

Training the Next Generation of Prophets

The Black Church has long been a cradle for prophetic leadership, nurturing individuals who articulate the struggles of their communities and chart a course toward justice and liberation. This tradition remains vital in addressing today's pressing challenges, including systemic racism, economic inequality, and social injustice. Young leaders are called to draw inspiration from the courage and resilience of historical figures like Rev. Pauli Murray and Rev. Joseph Lowery, who exemplified the Church's mission to advocate for the oppressed. Murray's trailblazing fight for gender and racial equality and Lowery's steadfast leadership in the Civil Rights Movement illuminate the enduring role of the Black Church as a powerful voice for justice.

One method of nurturing these voices is through structured mentorship within seminaries and church communities, creating environments where emerging leaders are grounded in the historical, theological, and social dimensions of Black prophetic ministry. Training in public speaking, advocacy, and community engagement equips these leaders with the skills needed to navigate the intersections of faith and activism, empowering them to become modern-day prophets capable of addressing contemporary injustices.

Providing Support and Resources for Emerging Leaders

To sustain the prophetic voice of the Black Church, it is essential to invest in resources and support systems for emerging leaders. Historically, the Black Church has been a wellspring of resources for community empowerment, providing both material and spiritual support. This institutional support enabled Black leaders to organize and lead campaigns across towns and cities, advocating for civil rights and social justice in the face of fierce opposition (Spencer, 2022).

Today's leaders benefit from similar institutional backing—whether through funding for community initiatives, access to educational opportunities, or platforms that amplify their voices. The Black Church's role as a resource-rich institution endows pastors and activists with social capital, enabling them to influence local and national conversations on critical issues affecting Black communities. This commitment to equipping leaders underscores the Black Church's role as a persistent force for justice, fostering the growth of new prophets who can rise to meet the challenges of today's social landscape (Spencer, 2022).

The Church as a Symbol of Hope for the Future

The prophetic mission of the Black Church goes beyond addressing immediate injustices; it is a vision of enduring hope and transformation. Rooted in the belief that all individuals are created equal before God, the Black Church preaches a message of dignity, justice, and respect for all. This call to "love thy neighbor" is not only a moral imperative but a practical pathway toward societal healing and unity (Perkins, 2019). By fostering this eschatological vision—an ultimate goal of a just and equitable world—the Black Church sustains and inspires its congregants to pursue liberation for themselves and others.

Sustaining the Vision of Justice and Equality

The Black Church's vision of justice and equality serves as both a moral compass and a rallying cry, guiding congregants to challenge oppression wherever it arises. This commitment is not a passive hope but an active pursuit of justice—an unyielding march toward freedom that has sustained Black communities through generations. As Rev. William Barber II has emphasized, justice must transcend mere aspiration and become a moral revolution that addresses racial inequities alongside economic and social injustices (Barber & Wilson-Hartgrove, 2016).

This commitment to justice echoes the historic social gospel of Black theology, which interprets salvation as liberation not only from personal sin but from the oppressive forces that pervade society. It is a call to collective accountability, urging believers to confront the structures that perpetuate inequality and to fight for a world that reflects the love and justice of God. In this way, the Black Church serves as an anchor, holding firmly to the values of justice and equality in a world often fraught with inequality.

Empowering Congregants to Carry the Prophetic Tradition Forward

The strength of the Black Church lies not only in its leaders but in the active participation of its congregants. As the Church reclaims its prophetic mission, it calls upon every member to play a part in this work of change. Lay members, or "prophets in the pews," are encouraged to take up roles within their communities, using their gifts and everyday influence to advocate for justice and equality in ways that are meaningful to their unique contexts. This approach democratizes the prophetic tradition, allowing the Church's mission to be carried forward by all who are inspired to act.

Empowering congregants to carry this mission forward means fostering a deep sense of ownership within the Church community. By encouraging community-led initiatives and fostering spaces for congregants to express their concerns and ideas, the Church nurtures a prophetic spirit that permeates every level of its structure. This "standpoint" approach, which mobilizes community resources against systemic injustices, transforms the prophetic mission into a collective pursuit, underscoring the Church's role as a moral force rooted in communal action.

Imagining a World of Dignity and Respect for All

At the heart of the Black Church's prophetic tradition is a vision of a world where dignity, respect, and justice are accessible to all. This eschatological hope, grounded in the teachings of Christ, compels the Church to fight not only for its members but for a world that upholds the worth of every individual. The prophetic tradition calls for a worldwide fellowship that rises above tribal, racial, social, and national barriers and expresses a love that unites rather than divides humanity.

In this pursuit of a just society, the Black Church offers more than spiritual guidance; it offers a blueprint for systemic transformation. By instilling a sense of dignity and self-worth in its congregants, the Church empowers them to advocate for their rights and to uplift others. This shared vision of dignity and equality resonates deeply within Black communities, reinforcing the Black Church's role as a cultural and spiritual anchor that continuously nurtures a collective commitment to justice, hope, and resilience (Everett, 2012; Spencer, 2022).

In its response to modern movements like Black Lives Matter, the Church demonstrates that the prophetic tradition is as relevant today as it was in the days of Dr. King and Nat Turner. By nurturing new prophetic voices, providing resources for emerging leaders, and empowering its congregants, the Black Church not only preserves its legacy but propels it forward.

As we confront today's challenges—racism, economic disparity, and mass incarceration—the Black Church's prophetic mission remains a guiding force, offering a vision of a world where all people are treated with dignity and respect. Through this enduring commitment to justice, the Church calls upon each of us to be agents of change, honoring the legacy of those who came before us and ensuring that the prophetic witness of the Church continues to be a powerful force for transformation in our communities and beyond.

7

Creating Sacred Space for Healing and Empowerment

As touched on previously, the Black Church has always served as a sacred, restorative haven for generations of African Americans—a place where healing, empowerment, and spiritual rejuvenation flourish amidst a world often marked by struggle and adversity (Lincoln & Mamiya, 1990). This unique role is profoundly significant when we consider the historical and ongoing challenges that Black communities face: systemic racism, economic hardship, and social exclusion. Within the walls of the Black Church, individuals have historically found not only refuge but also solidarity, strength, and a deep sense of purpose.

The Black Church embodies an ancient wisdom that speaks to the heart of survival, resilience, and hope. In this sacred space, worshippers are given the chance to lay down their burdens, find strength through collective prayer, and feel seen and heard within a community that understands their struggles intimately. African American spirituality is embedded in the human experience, encompassing both divine reference and the very tangible challenges of earthly life. This chapter explores the multifaceted ways in which the Black Church serves as a sacred space, both within its physical walls and throughout broader society via outreach, activism, and dedicated care.

To truly appreciate the transformational role of the Black Church, we must examine it not only as a building but as a lifeline that extends deep into community life, bridging the spiritual and the practical. This sacred space is one where trauma is acknowledged, resilience is fostered, and individuals are empowered to overcome adversity. By providing counseling, promoting mental health, and offering communal support, the Church has become an invaluable source of healing for Black communities, both historically and today.

Sacred Space: Ark of Healing

The Black Church has long been a sacred home of hope and endurance, a place where faith and heritage come together to uplift the African American community. Within its walls, we find the spiritual treasures and cultural legacy of a people who have overcome adversity time and again. The Black Church is holy ground where burdens are eased, spirits are refreshed, and communities are fortified.

Formed by the faith and determination of those who refused to surrender to despair, the Church stands as a living testimony to God's faithfulness. From the early days of slavery, Black slaves found safety, identity, community, refuge, and support through gatherings in church. These gatherings gave our ancestors not only refuge but also a renewed sense of purpose and a vision for a future centered on justice and equity. From the brutalities of slavery through the victories of the Civil Rights Movement, and now in our continuing quest for equality, the Black Church has held fast through every trial.

Much like the Ark of the Covenant once reminded the Israelites of God's steadfast presence, the Black Church serves as a spiritual anchor for its people. Here, we come together to grieve, rejoice, and draw strength, trusting that God is with us in every season. Yet the Church's calling runs deeper than symbolism. It is a living mission. Chandler (2017) boldly states that the Black Church's work "supersedes a mere check-off obligation of Christian duty" (p. 179). Indeed, it is a covenant of active love, committed to healing the brokenhearted, binding the wounded, and empowering the oppressed.

This holy charge is not just about offering refuge; it's about creating an environment where resilience is nurtured, stories of survival are shared, and each generation sparks hope for the next. While the Ark of the Covenant signaled God's nearness to the Israelites, the Black Church represents God's promises carried out in real time—summoning its community to rise above every challenge and live into the promise of freedom and triumph.

Let the Black Church remain this sacred space: a dwelling where every life is valued, every testimony is cherished, and every soul finds renewal. By holding true to this calling, the Church not only sustains its heritage but also honors the God who accompanies us through every valley and storm, offering steady hope for the road ahead.

Cultural Resilience and Historical Context

The architecture and design of African American churches reflect a deep cultural resilience, rooted in the Afrocentric duality of the natural and communal. The first Black church houses, built as early as the 18th century, embodied the community's desire for control and self-determination. These were more than mere buildings; they were "communal homes" where individuals could gather, organize, and express their faith without restraint (Hunter, 2022, p. 252). Chandler (2017) notes that "the early origins of the Black Church were born through these clandestine worship meetings" (p. 163). This legacy of resilience has been preserved through generations, as seen in churches like Emanuel African Methodist Episcopal Church, which remains a symbol of resistance and strength from slavery to the Civil Rights Movement and beyond. Despite facing threats of violence and destruction, such churches have persisted, embodying an endurance that reflects the strength and spirit of the community.

For many, these churches represent a sanctuary—a place not only to worship but to connect with cultural roots and foster resilience against external adversities. Spiritual songs cultivated a deep sense of transcendence that shaped the lives of these believers and gave them the inner strength and perseverance needed to endure suffering and remain steadfast in their faith. The architecture of Black churches reflects this cultural depth by symbolizing community aspirations through steeples reaching skyward and sanctuaries embodying security and aspiration.

Intersections of Faith, Culture, and Identity

The Black Church is a cultural epicenter that reinforces and celebrates Black identity. This intersection of faith, culture, and identity is essential to the Black Church's role as a source of empowerment. As spaces that affirm Afrocentric and Christian values, Black churches embrace elements that speak to the cultural and historical experiences of Black congregants. The presence of choir lofts and gospel music in services exemplifies the central role of music as an expression of faith and identity within the Black Church. These spaces tell the story of a community that has preserved its unique identity through faith and resilience.

The physical space of the church takes on deeper meaning when it becomes a living reflection of the community's identity and shared faith. The physicality of the church represents the transformative power of Black churches as communal anchors, embodying the spirit and strength of the people they represent. By fostering empowerment and a legacy that endures, Black churches serve as sacred spaces where faith, culture, and identity intersect to strengthen the community.

Addressing Anger and Depression: A Call to Black Church Leaders

Across the African American community, anger and depression have become deeply personal and collective burdens, often carried quietly yet influencing every facet of life. These aren't just individual struggles; they reflect a shared experience shaped by racial discrimination and systemic barriers. If we are to support, heal, and empower our people, we must first understand the roots and impacts of these challenges.

Racial Discrimination: A Constant Source of Stress

For African Americans, racial discrimination is not a rare occurrence but a regular, often daily reality. This enduring experience of racism creates a unique form of stress that takes both physical and emotional tolls. As sociologist Chavella T. Pittman (2011) notes, racial discrimination can trigger "chronic and acute forms of racial stress, leading to health-related problems" (p. 1110). These aren't fleeting encounters; they leave lasting marks, accumulating over time to impact mental and physical health alike. As stress compounds, it manifests in conditions like hypertension, anxiety, depression, and other psychological afflictions (p. 1110).

Coping Mechanisms: Cultural Responses to Racial Stress

African Americans have developed diverse coping strategies rooted in cultural resilience and shared history. Broadly, these strategies can be divided into active and passive responses. Active coping involves directly addressing stressors, whether through speaking out against injustice or taking action. Passive responses may involve avoidance or internalizing emotions. Pittman (2011) explains, "Active coping strategies are those that address the source of stress, while passive strategies are those that do not" (p. 1112). For many, the choice between confronting or absorbing racial stress is influenced by the need to balance emotional resilience with self-preservation.

This balance becomes even more delicate when anger is the primary response. Anger is natural and, in the face of injustice, often justified. Yet, without a constructive outlet or healing strategy, anger can start to harm the very people it's meant to protect.

The Hidden Cost of Anger on Mental Health

Anger serves as a powerful and often immediate response to the injustice that African Americans face. However, research suggests that anger, when consistently used as the main coping tool, can take a heavy toll on mental health. Pittman (2011) found that those who cope with discrimination by using active anger often report lower levels of well-being and experience greater psychological distress. "Participants who used active anger to cope with acute racial discrimination had significantly lower well-being scores than those who did not" (p. 1119). This finding highlights the importance of providing alternative methods of coping that don't inadvertently worsen mental health struggles.

Additionally, factors such as household size and education level can influence how anger is managed. In larger households, where stress levels may be elevated, individuals might find themselves more susceptible to expressing anger. As Pittman (2011) points out, "The confluence of the increased stress and reduced mental health associated with larger households might contribute to individuals losing their temper" (p. 1122). This context is vital for community leaders as they consider approaches that address specific needs within diverse family structures.

Rethinking Anger: A Call for Compassionate Coping

Pittman's study invites us to reconsider the reliance on anger as a primary way of coping with racism. While anger is a valid and sometimes necessary reaction, it also carries risks if it remains unresolved or unchanneled. Pittman (2011) cautions, "These findings ... raise concerns about the effectiveness (or lack thereof) of anger as a common coping mechanism for racism, given the deleterious effects it may have on African Americans' mental health" (p. 1122). This challenges us, as leaders, to promote coping mechanisms that honor the community's experience while supporting mental resilience and long-term stability.

The Black Church as a Lifeline
Amidst Adversity

The Black Church has been the primary institution for social support and healing within African American communities, particularly in the face of systemic adversity. In fact, the Church has long served as the backbone of the Black community, an institution that fosters cultural resilience, spiritual empowerment, and community solidarity. This foundation has historically enabled the Black Church to function as a bastion against the dehumanizing effects of oppression, creating a space where Black identity, cultural heritage, and spiritual life are protected and celebrated. For centuries, the Black Church has offered a sanctuary where congregants can find solace, release their burdens, and engage in worship practices that affirm their worth and dignity in a world that often challenges both.

This legacy of resilience is not just rooted in individual survival but in collective healing, a unique feature that distinguishes the Black Church as a "sacred space" where empowerment is both personal and communal (Hunter, 2022). From worship services filled with songs of hope to sermons that ignite a sense of purpose, the Black Church creates an environment where individuals can find spiritual, emotional, and even physical healing through shared experiences and faith-based practices.

The Church's Response to Trauma and Mental Health Needs

Trauma is a prevalent experience in Black communities due to centuries of enslavement, segregation, discrimination, and ongoing social and economic challenges. The Black Church has served as a provider of informal social services, offering preventive and treatment-oriented programs that promote the psychological well-being of congregants (Blank et al. (2002)). These initiatives highlight the Church's commitment to addressing the root causes of trauma, such as economic inequality, violence, and social injustice, through community-centered support and healing practices. By fostering a safe space where individuals can confront their pain within a supportive and understanding environment, the Black Church continues its legacy of healing.

The Black Church also provides a vital bridge between spiritual care and professional mental health resources. Recognizing the stigma often associated with mental health in the community, many Black churches have adopted counseling services, support groups, and partnerships with mental health professionals to promote holistic well-being. This integrated approach enables the Church to meet the psychological needs of its members while maintaining its commitment to spiritual care. It also serves as a foundation for mental health literacy and advocacy within the Black community, helping to destigmatize mental health issues and encourage individuals to seek the support they need.

Sacred Spaces Beyond the Church Walls: Outreach and Activism

Beyond the physical church building, the Black Church extends its sacred mission through outreach and community service, embodying the spirit of a faith that is active in meeting the needs of the people. Programs aimed at feeding the hungry, providing shelter for the homeless, and offering resources for those struggling with addiction underscore the Church's role as an entity that serves the entire community, not just its congregants. These acts of service reflect a commitment to communal well-being that has been at the heart of the Black Church since its inception.

As Brewer and Williams (2019) note, the sacred space created by Black churches offers a foundation for solidarity and cultural resilience. By stepping beyond its walls and into the lives of those in need, the Black Church fulfills its mission of being a healing presence in the world. For example, many Black churches run food pantries, clothing drives, and community kitchens that provide essential services to vulnerable populations. These programs are not merely acts of charity; they are acts of empowerment, as they restore dignity, provide essential support, and help individuals rebuild their lives with a sense of purpose and belonging. By offering these services, the Church ensures that its commitment to support is both holistic and inclusive. For instance, these efforts not only meet immediate needs but also inspire congregants and community members to see the Church as a living embodiment of healing and transformation. In offering such essential services, the Black Church transforms city streets and community centers into extensions of the sanctuary itself, reinforcing that the sacredness of the Church extends wherever there is a need for comfort, dignity, and hope (Gilliard, 2020).

The Call to Continue the Legacy

In a society that continues to present challenges for Black communities, the role of the Black Church as a sacred space for healing and empowerment remains as vital as ever. This sacred space extends beyond brick and mortar, manifesting in the hearts and actions of its congregants, who embody the Church's mission in their daily lives. The Black Church has shown that it is possible to create a sanctuary not only within its physical structure but also within the collective soul of its people, inspiring resilience, unity, and a commitment to justice.

As we reflect on the transformational power of the Black Church, we are reminded of the importance of nurturing this legacy for future generations. The call to foster healing, advocate for justice, and support mental well-being is not just a historical role but a contemporary necessity. Through this chapter, we aim to inspire readers to consider how they can contribute to this mission, whether by supporting community initiatives, addressing mental health needs, or simply by standing in solidarity with the Black Church's mission of creating sacred spaces for all who seek refuge.

The Black Church as a Physical Sanctuary

The Black Church has long served as a haven—physically, emotionally, and spiritually—for communities facing societal challenges. The Black Church is a place where every life is treasured, every story is sacred, and every soul is renewed by the power of God's presence. In many ways, the Black Church mirrors the Ark of the Covenant for its congregants: a sacred vessel brimming with divine strength that safeguards both the spirit and collective identity of a people confronted by marginalization (Lincoln & Mamiya, 1990; Spurgeon, 1895).

Significance of the Church Building as Sacred Space

For those who have endured displacement and discrimination, the very walls of the Black Church symbolize security and belonging. Throughout the African American experience, these sanctuaries provided space to gather, pray, and organize—places free from the social barriers that kept Black communities on the margins. During slavery, segregation, and Jim Crow, they were among the few spots where African Americans could meet without constant scrutiny or fear of retaliation (Wilmore, 1998). Within these sacred walls, people discovered their humanity, dignity, and collective strength.

Yet the sanctuary is more than a physical refuge. It supports a shared identity, one forged by common experiences and strengthened by deep spiritual roots. These walls have witnessed both celebration and sorrow, each pew and pulpit telling a story of endurance amid oppression. As Chandler (2017) and Brewer and Williams (2019) note, the physical church building represents the intersection of the divine and everyday life, offering congregants an enduring sense of community and spiritual security.

In this way, the Black Church building is not merely a house of worship—it stands as a foundation of identity and perseverance. Just as the Ark of the Covenant reminded the Israelites of God's continual presence, the church edifice testifies to the enduring protection of God, where the community's shared spirit continues to thrive (Hunter, 2022).

Collective Worship and Emotional Support

The power of collective worship in the Black Church lies in its ability to transform personal grief and joy into a communal experience of healing and strength. Worship in this context is more than individual devotion; it is a shared ritual that connects each congregant's story to a larger narrative. Within the sanctuary, songs and sermons become vehicles of emotional catharsis and empowerment. Here, worship is both a balm for personal wounds and a rallying cry for collective resilience (Brewer & Williams, 2019).

Through worship, congregants engage in a form of communal therapy, where the act of gathering amplifies each individual's faith and strengthens their resolve. Music, with its deep roots in African American culture, plays a key role in worship. The rhythms of spirituals, hymns, and gospel songs speak to shared histories of pain and triumph, linking past struggles to present-day aspirations for justice and hope. Congregational singing, especially the call-and-response exchanges between preacher and congregation, creates a dynamic flow of energy that empowers each person in the room (Mattis & Grayman-Simpson, 2013).

The sermons, too, are crafted to address both personal and collective experiences of the congregants. They are often rich with themes of endurance, divine justice, and the triumph of good over evil. For people facing personal trials or systemic discrimination, these messages offer guidance and reassurance, reminding them that they are not alone in their struggles. Through words, music, and communal presence, the Black Church transforms the act of worship into an essential form of emotional support and resilience-building.

Shared Emotional Experiences and Community Bonding

One of the most profound aspects of the Black Church is its role in fostering shared emotional experiences, which are essential for building a strong community. The church is a space where people come together to celebrate, mourn, and share life's milestones in a supportive environment. These shared experiences—whether a baptism, wedding, funeral, or community prayer service—reinforce the bonds between congregants, creating a "family" bound not just by faith but by a common history and shared values (Hunter, 2022).

Rituals in the Black Church, such as communal mourning and celebratory rites, help to shape a collective identity rooted in shared resilience. When a member of the congregation passes away, for example, the community gathers to celebrate their life and offer support to the grieving family. Funeral services are not merely a time of mourning; they are a testament to the deceased's life and the impact they had on their community. Through shared prayers, singing, and testimonies, congregants collectively bear the weight of loss, transforming individual grief into a moment of communal solidarity (Brewer & Williams, 2019).

Similarly, rites of passage such as baptisms, weddings, and child dedications are celebrated with fervor and joy, marking the importance of each life stage within the context of community. These gatherings are moments of joy and renewal, reinforcing the interconnectedness of congregants and affirming the collective strength of the Church. The communal nature of these experiences fosters a deep sense of belonging, helping individuals feel that they are part of something larger than themselves—a resilient and loving community (Mattis & Grayman-Simpson, 2013).

Emotional and Psychological Healing Through Community Support

Healing in the Black Church extends beyond the spiritual realm to include emotional and psychological well-being. The trauma that many Black Americans face—from historical injustices like slavery and segregation to modern challenges such as police violence, economic inequality, and health disparities—can be overwhelming. The Church serves as a safe space where these traumas can be addressed openly, allowing individuals to find solace and strength within a community that understands their struggles.

The act of coming together in worship and fellowship provides a powerful means of psychological support. Sermons and songs often include themes of divine justice and redemption, reminding congregants that they are not alone in their suffering and that, through faith, they can find healing. These messages help congregants process their pain and anger by turning what might be a source of despair into a renewed sense of purpose and hope.

Moreover, the Black Church fosters mental health by encouraging the sharing of personal testimonies. Congregants are often invited to speak about their struggles and triumphs, offering a cathartic release and an opportunity for others to find hope in shared experiences. This communal approach to healing breaks down the stigma around discussing mental health, making it more acceptable to seek help and support within the church environment. By addressing emotional and psychological needs, the Black Church continues to serve as an essential support system, one that upholds the well-being of its members in every aspect of their lives (Brewer & Williams, 2019; Wilmore, 1998).

The Black Church's Role in Promoting Healing and Mental Health

For generations, the Black Church has been a sanctuary of spiritual and emotional support. Now, in the face of growing mental health challenges, it must again rise to meet the needs of its people. Church leaders are uniquely positioned to address these issues, to foster open dialogues about mental health, and to encourage strategies that support well-being rather than strain it. By creating a safe space where mental health struggles are acknowledged and resources are offered, the Black Church can continue its legacy of healing and hope.

It's clear that more research and targeted interventions are needed to fully support our community's mental health needs. Addressing the unique challenges of coping with racism requires focused study and the development of culturally informed strategies that promote healing and long-term well-being. Partnerships with mental health professionals, workshops, and support groups within the Church could be transformative in helping individuals learn to manage their anger and resilience more constructively.

Addressing the mental health challenges faced by our community requires a careful balance between righteous anger and sustainable coping. As we look forward, let us move with compassion and wisdom, dedicating ourselves to the well-being of those we serve. By coming together, the Black Church can create a supportive community that not only endures hardship but also builds the strength to flourish.

Black Church Leadership: A Pathway to Genuine Mental Health Support

The issue of mental health within the African American community presents a profound challenge, requiring a dedicated and compassionate response from Black church leaders. To make a genuine difference, church leaders must move beyond superficial approaches and delve into the complexities of mental health with insight and intentionality. Understanding the historical role of the Black Church as both a sanctuary and a social resource is key. Black churches have been the bedrock of African American life since the days of slavery, offering a place of refuge and empowerment when societal institutions failed to support the community's needs (Dempsey, et al., 2016). Today, as mental health issues continue to rise, the Black Church is positioned to address these needs in a way that is culturally resonant and deeply impactful.

Unaddressed Mental Health Needs and Historical Mistrust

African Americans experience higher rates of untreated mental health conditions than any other racial group in the United States, underscoring a serious disparity in mental health access and care (Dempsey et al., 2016). This crisis is rooted in various factors, including economic barriers, limited access to healthcare, and a historical mistrust of formal mental health institutions. Due to the legacy of institutional racism, many African Americans are understandably hesitant to seek help from agencies perceived as external to their community. This "cultural mistrust" acts as a powerful deterrent, often leading African Americans to view mental health services with suspicion, particularly when there is a lack of cultural alignment between the client and the clinician (Dempsey et al., 2016). The Black Church, however, has the potential to bridge this divide by providing mental health support that is both accessible and culturally affirming.

Clergy as Counselors: Trusted Yet Limited

On the other hand, seeking help from church leaders offers "cultural comfort," as clergy are familiar with the unique challenges of their community and share in its values and experiences (Dempsey et al., 2016, p. 78). Unlike many external mental health professionals, church leaders are already embedded within the community, which fosters a sense of trust and understanding. However, most clergy are not equipped with the clinical training required to address complex mental health issues comprehensively. This limitation poses a significant challenge; while clergy can offer emotional and spiritual support, they may not have the skills to address conditions like depression, trauma, or anxiety effectively (p. 79).

Building Partnerships with Mental Health Professionals

To make a meaningful impact, Black church leaders must consider collaborating with mental health professionals to create a holistic approach that encompasses both spiritual guidance and clinical expertise. Partnerships between Black churches and mental health agencies have shown promise in the past, highlighting the potential for effective collaboration when both sides are committed to cultural understanding. For instance, Dempsey et al. (2016) found that church leaders who had close relationships with senior pastors advocating for mental health services were more open to aligning their support with outside agencies. By building trust with mental health professionals and integrating them into the church community, Black church leaders can provide congregants with comprehensive resources that address both their spiritual and mental health needs.

Transformative Roles for Clergy: Training and Awareness

To expand their influence in mental health advocacy, clergy can benefit from targeted training that equips them to recognize mental health issues and refer individuals to appropriate resources. With such training, clergy could serve as an essential first line of support, identifying when congregants may need more specialized care and fostering an environment where seeking mental health support is encouraged rather than stigmatized. Additionally, training in culturally responsive counseling would help clergy provide support that respects the nuances of African American experiences with mental health, allowing them to act as informed intermediaries who can bridge the gap between congregants and mental health professionals.

For collaborative efforts to be truly successful, mental health professionals must also approach these partnerships with an understanding of Black church culture. As Dempsey et al. (2016) emphasize, "An adequate assessment must be conducted to understand church culture, etiquette, and protocol" (p. 82). When counselors respect the church's culture and engage in ways that resonate with its practices and values, they can gain the trust of the congregation and provide support that feels genuine and respectful.

Community-Centered Mental Health Initiatives

Black churches have the unique ability to integrate mental health discussions into existing church activities in a way that feels organic and non-threatening. By incorporating mental health awareness into community events, Bible study sessions, and even sermons, church leaders can address these issues directly, normalizing conversations around mental health. According to Dempsey et al. (2016), engaging mental health professionals in church-led health fairs, workshops, and support groups offers an effective, community-centered way to introduce these resources (p. 83). This approach allows mental health professionals to engage the congregation where they are, fostering a sense of collaboration that is non-intrusive and culturally appropriate.

Embracing the Future: A Vision of Holistic Well-Being

The future of mental health support within the Black Church lies in an integrated model that combines faith with evidence-based mental health practices. Black church leaders have the opportunity to redefine mental health advocacy within their communities, transforming the Church into a space where emotional and psychological well-being are as valued as spiritual health. This holistic approach, rooted in cultural understanding and trust, can help dismantle the stigma around mental health and empower African Americans to seek the support they deserve.

As leaders consider their role in addressing these challenges, they are called not only to support but also to actively champion mental health within the framework of faith. Through meaningful collaborations, culturally sensitive training, and community-centered initiatives, the Black Church can continue its legacy of healing and empowerment, offering sanctuary for both the soul and the mind.

8

The Future of the Black Church and Its Covenant

As DISCUSSED THROUGHOUT THIS BOOK, THE BLACK Church has long served as a beacon of resilience and a sanctuary for Black communities, offering both spiritual guidance and a foundation for social empowerment. As Du Bois (1903) poignantly described, the Church remains a vessel for communal uplift, fostering a sacred space that reinforces spiritual resilience and preserves cultural identity. Even though it was written in 1903, this still holds truth today:

> The Negro church of to-day is the social centre of Negro life in the United States, and the most characteristic expression of African character. ... This building is the central club-house of a community.... Various organizations meet here, the church proper, the Sunday-school,

> two or three insurance societies,
> women's societies, secret societies,
> and mass meetings of various kinds.
> ... The church often stands as a real
> conserver of morals, a strengthener
> of family life, and the final authority
> on what is Good and Right. (Du Bois
> 1903, p. 101)

This vision of the Black Church as a sacred vessel underscores its dual role as both a guardian of Black heritage and a wellspring of community resilience. Through its teachings, rituals, and activism, the Church serves as a repository for collective memory and a vision of hope for the future. While its historic role echoes the symbolic significance of the Ark of the Covenant as a testament to divine presence and promise, the Church's mission is both rooted in cultural preservation and forward-looking in its approach to justice and empowerment.

Safeguarding these core values requires the Black Church to embrace the evolving demands of a modern era. McIntosh and Curry (2020) highlight the importance of adapting church leadership and outreach to reflect contemporary calls for inclusion, intersectionality, and innovative approaches to advocacy. In this way, the Church's mission remains grounded in its historical foundations while expanding to meet the spiritual and social needs of a diverse and shifting congregation. By blending its rich legacy with a vision for the future, the Black Church ensures that it continues to be a vital source of strength, perseverance, and unity for its community.

The purpose of this chapter is to envision a path forward for the Black Church, one that respects its rich history while embracing the necessary evolution for future growth. The Church's enduring mission to empower, educate, and uplift has positioned it as a "rock" within Black communities. The Church has been a foundation upon which generations have built their sense of identity and belonging. As a communal institution, the Church must continue to hold the values that have sustained it while fostering a culture that embraces new voices and innovative approaches. This chapter addresses key areas where the Black Church can expand its impact, from developing intergenerational leadership to embracing inclusivity, leveraging technology, and empowering future leaders through theological education.

Intergenerational Leadership: Bridging the Generational Gap

The future of the Black Church relies significantly on cultivating robust intergenerational leadership. As a sacred vessel for community resilience, the Church must integrate both the wisdom of its elders and the innovative ideas of its youth, forming a cohesive vision that propels it into the future. Such unity, achieved through mentorship, knowledge transfer, and the acceptance of new perspectives, establishes a foundation that not only honors the Church's historical legacy but also ensures its adaptability in an evolving world (Smith & Snell, 2009).

Fostering Mentorship and Knowledge Transfer

Within the Black Church, mentorship is more than an educational tool; it is a bridge that connects generations, allowing for an exchange of wisdom, values, and experiences essential for sustaining the Church's mission. Programs such as youth councils, elder-led mentorship initiatives, and cross-generational worship create spaces where younger congregants can learn from those who came before them, gaining insights into the challenges and triumphs that have shaped their community. This exchange is not merely functional; it is a reaffirmation of identity and shared purpose. Mentorship within the Black Church functions as a vital bridge, linking the wisdom and lived experience of older generations with the passion, creativity, and fresh perspectives of younger generations.

Through mentorship, elders impart both historical context and personal wisdom. They stand as living testimonies to the faith and fortitude that have sustained the Church through generations of adversity. Youth councils and leadership training programs provide structured avenues for younger members to engage with their elders, fostering an environment of mutual respect and understanding. The relationship between elders and youth is vital because sharing life experiences and spiritual insight nurtures resilience and guides younger generations to face challenges with faith and steadfast conviction. This reciprocal engagement nurtures a robust community that values both tradition and progress, preparing the younger generation to assume leadership roles while preserving the foundational principles of the Church.

Embracing New Perspectives and Innovations

As the Church moves forward, it faces the challenge of remaining relevant in an increasingly diverse and digitally connected world. Embracing new perspectives, especially those of younger members, is vital for ensuring that the Church's mission resonates with contemporary society. As previously discussed, by integrating modern practices such as digital outreach, social media engagement, and contemporary worship styles, the Church demonstrates an openness to innovation that is crucial for engaging a younger audience. McIntosh and Curry (2020) note that integrating modern technology into worship strengthens engagement across generations, drawing in younger members while helping the Black Church remain vibrant, connected, and relevant within an ever-evolving digital culture.

Leadership summits and digital media training programs equip the younger generation with skills that enhance their capacity to lead effectively while remaining anchored in the Church's mission. This openness to new ideas reflects the Church's commitment to inclusivity, as it recognizes the value each generation brings to its communal life. Cross-generational worship plays a crucial role within the Black Church by strengthening communal bonds and creating meaningful opportunities for mentorship, mutual understanding, and shared spiritual growth across all ages. This flexibility allows the Church to address complex issues facing Black communities today, from social justice to economic empowerment, while maintaining its spiritual integrity and historical legacy.

By embracing fresh perspectives, the Church transforms itself into a space that honors both legacy and progress. This adaptability is not a departure from its roots but rather an expansion of its mission, creating an institution that evolves alongside the needs of its members (J. Williams et al., 2019). Each generation brings unique strengths, and by inviting young leaders to participate actively, the Church reinforces its role as a vibrant, living community that adapts to the times without losing sight of its core values.

Building a Foundation for Future Leaders

To ensure its long-term vitality, the Black Church must invest in the structured education and spiritual formation of its future leaders. Black theological schools and Church-based educational institutions play a pivotal role in this preparation, offering not only doctrinal training but also grounding in the cultural and historical contexts that shape the Black Church's identity. These institutions serve as learning centers where emerging leaders gain a foundation in spiritual practice, community service, and the practical skills necessary for ministry.

Educational institutions like seminaries create an environment in which future pastors and leaders can explore the theological, ethical, and social dimensions of their roles. This grounding enables new leaders to approach their responsibilities with a respect for tradition and a willingness to innovate. Education serves as both a pathway to personal growth and a cornerstone of collective progress, fostering dignity, empowerment, and the advancement of the entire community. This conviction aligns closely with the Church's mission to uplift and sustain its community.

Theological institutions emphasize a balance between tradition and innovation, preparing leaders who understand the complexities of their communities and can adapt to new challenges while upholding the Church's core principles. Preparing future leaders within the Black Church involves honoring the wisdom of the past while cultivating openness to fresh ideas. This generational development of leadership ensures that theological education remains both rooted and forward-looking. By fostering mentorship, embracing modern approaches, and supporting the theological education of future leaders, the Black Church strengthens its foundation and equips itself to carry its mission forward.

Creating a Culture of Inclusivity and Belonging

For the Black Church to remain a sanctuary of hope and a catalyst for justice, it must also deepen its commitment to inclusivity and diversity. This involves intentionally creating spaces where all voices are valued, and all members feel seen and heard. Historically, the Church has been a place of refuge and solidarity, but the future demands an even broader embrace—welcoming marginalized groups, affirming the experiences of women, and addressing generational shifts with empathy and understanding.

As scholars like McIntosh and Curry (2020) argue, inclusivity strengthens the Church's mission by fostering unity in diversity, ensuring that its covenant of faith reflects the fullness of God's love and justice. The Church's call is to embody these principles in practice, becoming a true sanctuary where everyone is empowered to contribute, worship, and lead. By moving beyond barriers and amplifying the voices of those historically left out, the Black Church can remain a vibrant and transformative institution, carrying its legacy of faith, justice, and love boldly into the future.

The Black Church as a Sanctuary of Inclusion and Resilience

For centuries, the Black Church has stood as a sacred space of spiritual refuge, a place where the collective struggle of Black Americans could find expression, validation, and resilience. Known for its deep roots in cultural preservation and social justice, the Black Church has been more than a place of worship; it has been a cornerstone of community resilience, a gathering point for strategizing, organizing, and fostering hope amid systemic oppression. However, despite its outward mission of justice, the Church has historically faced internal challenges regarding inclusivity. Leadership roles have often been reserved for a select demographic, sidelining women, young people, and other marginalized groups from decision-making positions.

Addressing these long-standing barriers is crucial for the Church's mission to remain relevant and resonant in an increasingly diverse and evolving society. The Black Church's pursuit of inclusivity reflects its core commitment to justice and its awareness of the need to grow with changing times. Every member is embraced within its spiritual and communal life. This call to adapt does not imply a departure from tradition but rather a return to the Church's core values of justice and love. By embracing diversity within its ranks, the Black Church can more effectively embody the inclusivity it advocates and serve as a fuller reflection of the community it represents.

Expanding Leadership: Dismantling Exclusionary Practices

To fulfill its mission authentically, the Black Church must confront and dismantle the exclusionary practices that have historically restricted leadership opportunities for certain groups. Overcoming these barriers requires a proactive commitment to creating pathways for women, young people, and other marginalized groups to take on meaningful leadership roles. This inclusive approach is not only an ethical imperative but also a strategic one; by empowering these voices, the Church reinforces its foundational commitment to equality and justice, cultivating a leadership structure that mirrors the diversity of its congregation.

This effort to diversify leadership is not just about representation but also about enriching the Church's mission. Each new perspective brought to the table enhances the Church's ability to address a broader spectrum of issues facing the community, from social justice advocacy to mental health support, ensuring that the Church remains a relevant force for good.

Spirituality as Sanctuary: The Role of Inclusive Spaces for Marginalized Youth

For many young individuals from marginalized communities, spirituality often becomes a sanctuary amid societal challenges. These youth, who may face systemic discrimination, economic hardship, or cultural misunderstandings, seek spaces that affirm their dignity and identity without judgment. Scholars like Barnes (2023) emphasize how spirituality, as opposed to rigid formalized religion, offers a flexible, personal refuge. This informal approach to faith allows young congregants to engage in spiritual practices that honor their lived experiences while fostering a sense of belonging. The open and nonjudgmental nature of such spirituality offers a vital place of refuge and guidance and provides the sense of safety and belonging needed during seasons of personal growth. Spirituality thus becomes a powerful tool for resilience and self-discovery, aligning with the Black Church's mission of justice and compassion.

By focusing on spirituality and inclusivity, the Black Church has an opportunity to create welcoming spaces for all marginalized youth. This approach underscores the Church's commitment to equity and the well-being of its entire congregation, ensuring that no one feels excluded. It empowers young people to see the Church as a community that values their unique contributions, fostering intergenerational connections that strengthen the Church's future. Such inclusivity is not just an act of compassion—it is an embodiment of the Church's broader mission to reflect God's love for all His children.

Generational Differences: Bridging Gaps in Church Attendance and Engagement

Generational divides within the Black Church highlight the need for adaptive strategies that resonate with younger congregants. Many younger believers are disengaging from traditional forms of worship and seeking expressions of faith that feel more authentic, inclusive, and relevant to their lived experiences. Many young Black Americans are seeking spiritual connections that extend beyond traditional worship and embrace a broader, more inclusive understanding of faith. These young congregants often view spirituality as an authentic, fluid expression of their beliefs, one that transcends rigid doctrinal boundaries and offers a personal connection to the divine. For these individuals, spirituality represents a more relevant and flexible approach to faith, one that meets them in their unique contexts and affirms their individuality.

In response, the Black Church can bridge generational gaps by creating spaces where younger voices feel valued and respected. Programs that incorporate technology, contemporary worship styles, and social justice initiatives can engage younger members and invite them into active participation. A church that listens to and learns from its youth is a church that remains alive, vibrant, and capable of navigating the complexities of an ever-evolving society.

Womanist Theology and the Role of Women in Leadership

The contributions of womanist theology emphasize the importance of affirming the experiences of Black women within the Church. Womanist theology underscores the unique resilience and insight that Black women bring to the spiritual community, often drawing from their lived experiences of overcoming adversity. Womanist theology elevates the voices of Black women by affirming their inherent worth and recognizing the enduring strength and faith that have sustained both them and their communities through generations. By embracing womanist perspectives, the Black Church can broaden its understanding of leadership and create opportunities for women to lead in ways that honor their unique strengths and experiences.

Expanding leadership to include women's voices is essential for fostering an environment of equality and empathy. This inclusivity reflects the Church's commitment to justice, ensuring that every congregant's voice is heard and valued. Women leaders bring perspectives that enrich the Church's ministry and deepen its commitment to social justice, community advocacy, and holistic well-being. Such inclusive practices underscore the transformative power of a church that genuinely represents the diversity of its members.

Creating a Community That Reflects All Members' Experiences

For the Black Church to grow and remain significant, it must make the voices of marginalized groups a part of its conversation. This is about more than just letting these groups have a seat at the leadership table; it is about creating an atmosphere where their voices and perspectives are respected and welcomed in making the decisions that affect the Church's mission and vision. This shift not only requires the Church to make room for kinds of within-group diversity that have too often been ignored—it also requires a commitment to policy and appearance changes that make the Church a less hostile and more welcoming environment for everyone who might want to advocate or use the Church as a platform for social justice.

The Black Church can better tackle the singular predicaments encountered by women and other historically marginalized people when it promotes them to leadership positions. This serves a dual purpose: (a) It diversifies ecclesiastical governance, and that is in itself a good thing. It respects and recognizes the unique characteristics—both positive and negative—that are associated with ministers and members who identify as part of these groups. (b) It sends a powerful message to the entire congregation: we are inclusive, everyone is valuable, and, more to the point, these characteristics make our Church and our community stronger (McIntosh & Curry, 2020).

Through its commitment to inclusivity, the Black Church models an approach to community that aligns with its spiritual and moral convictions, shaping both its internal and external influence. The Church's journey toward inclusivity is not only a necessary evolution but a fulfillment of its covenant with God—to be a place of refuge, justice, and hope for all.

Leveraging Technology for Growth and Engagement

In today's world, technology is reshaping the ways in which communities connect, worship, and communicate. For the Black Church, technology is not merely a tool but a bridge—expanding its reach, deepening connections, and opening doors to new ways of fulfilling its mission.

Social Media and Youth Engagement

Engaging with young people who see the Black Church as irrelevant is an emerging opportunity area for the Black Church. Although relics of a Black Church past may seem to be condemned, many of these young adults, when polled, still hold to some semblance of a faith. However, they do not see the organizational structure of the Black Church as something they want to engage with. Many in this generation do see an opportunity to "reclaim" the church, but a church stripped of the negative traditions and practices they associate with church life. If this is what the Black Church has to offer as it navigates the next decade, then "navigating" (rather than appearing to be "leading") may be the best course.

The Black Church cannot solely charge ahead with an agenda. It must also beckon the younger generations to what it offers. The Church can do this most effectively if it adopts a multifaceted and contemporary approach, which leverages the platforms of today and speaks the language of now. Instagram, X (formerly Twitter), and TikTok are all fair game. But not just any game—for the Church to win when reaching its young audience, it must share messages that are as good for the soul as they are for the selfie. This means content that is spiritually refreshing, sure, but also content that addresses the pressing concerns of the day and that, by the way, could use some more of the Church's touch. Social media has become a vital means of engaging youth in the Black Church by offering platforms where younger generations can connect, share, and express their faith in ways that feel genuine and personally meaningful.

In addition, social media can help young adults feel a sense of belonging and engagement. The Church operates on a model of "democracy," where individuals are included and valued. This participatory model not only enhances the sense of ownership but also reinforces the idea that the Church is a space for everyone to inhabit collectively.

Besides cultivating engagement, virtual church spaces can allow for equally innovative forms of worship and fellowship. Live-streamed services, virtual small groups, and interactive Bible studies can allow for a new kind of connection that those prayerful and worshipful events haven't really had before. You can gamify them now with the help of the Internet, even if only to keep the eyes of the participants fresh so that they don't doze off.

The main task for the Black Church is to convert how it's perceived. As social media becomes more and more of a part of life, we must embrace it as part of our lives. When you embrace something, you have to hug it close to you. Doing so gives the Black Church the chance to tell our story to a medium in which a large number of the audience is already captivated. It's vital for us to use this storytelling opportunity to ensure our narrative becomes a collective one. It needs to be a story of shared purpose and identity—an inclusive one that emphasizes that there's a space and a role in the Black Church for you, too, as well as a way of life lived out in many corners of this nation that doesn't shy away from saying it serves a purpose for as many people as possible. The growth of virtual ministry and online platforms is helping the Black Church reconnect with younger generations, demonstrating its adaptability and willingness to meet people where they are—both in their communities and in the digital spaces they inhabit.

Technological Advancements for Accessibility and Community Building

Advancements in technology have allowed the Black Church to create a more inclusive worship experience, addressing the needs of congregants who may face physical barriers to participation. For those with disabilities or social anxieties, online access provides a comfortable and inclusive alternative for engaging with their faith community. By integrating accessibility tools and offering virtual access to services, the Church extends its message of unity and support to all members, fulfilling its mission to be a sanctuary for everyone. Online accessibility tools allow the Black Church to include members who may face physical barriers to participation and provide a more inclusive worship experience.

Additionally, virtual platforms enable the formation of online communities that connect individuals across regions. Congregants who have relocated or live far from their home churches can still participate in services, join Bible study groups, and stay connected to their spiritual roots. These digital communities foster a sense of belonging and provide a support network for those who may otherwise feel disconnected. Such technological advancements allow the Black Church to embody the inclusivity and unity it seeks to promote, offering a model for how faith can be both a local and global experience.

Economic Empowerment and Financial Literacy

Economic empowerment has been a cornerstone of the Black Church's mission, providing the Black community with resources to navigate and overcome systemic economic challenges. From financial literacy to workforce training, the Church has offered practical support aimed at fostering self-sufficiency. However, as economic inequality continues to widen, particularly in Black communities, the Church is called to expand its role even further, embracing innovative methods to close the financial gaps that persist. The Church must continue to act as a vessel of hope and support, equipping its members with tools to achieve financial independence, stability, and ultimately, empowerment.

Addressing Economic Inequality Through Church Initiatives

Historically, the Black Church has been a vital force for economic empowerment, responding to community needs with a range of initiatives aimed at reducing economic inequality. These initiatives, such as financial literacy workshops, small business support, and workforce development programs, serve to provide congregants with essential skills and opportunities for financial growth. Such programs not only offer immediate support but also build long-term financial resilience within the community. Economic empowerment has long been central to the mission of the Black Church, serving as a pathway for African Americans to achieve stability, dignity, and independence within a society that has often limited their opportunities.

Financial literacy programs, in particular, equip congregants with skills to manage debt, save effectively, and invest in ways that promote generational wealth. These programs serve as foundational steps toward financial independence, especially for those who may lack access to traditional financial education. Financial literacy programs play a vital role in the Black Church's mission of economic empowerment by giving congregants the knowledge and tools needed to manage their resources wisely, build stability, and create lasting wealth. Furthermore, by addressing economic disparities at a local level, the Church reinforces the idea that economic justice is integral to its spiritual mission.

Additionally, workforce development initiatives provide vocational training, career counseling, and skill-building workshops, preparing individuals for sustainable employment. The Black Church, therefore, serves as a sanctuary not only for worship but also for economic growth, empowering its members to contribute positively to their communities and beyond. Through these initiatives, the Church reinforces the importance of self-reliance and resilience, echoing the teachings of economic empowerment that have shaped its mission for generations.

Church Partnerships With Local Businesses and Financial Institutions

In its mission to promote economic stability, the Black Church has increasingly recognized the importance of partnering with local businesses and financial institutions. These partnerships create access to resources that might otherwise remain out of reach for many in the community. By collaborating with banks, credit unions, and local entrepreneurs, the Church can facilitate programs that provide congregants with financial counseling, loans for small businesses, and additional support for economic advancement. Through partnerships with local banks, Black churches are able to strengthen small businesses associated with their congregations by expanding access to capital and resources that might otherwise remain out of reach.

Such partnerships empower the Church to act as a bridge between community members and essential financial resources, fostering entrepreneurship and promoting financial independence. Small-business grants, low-interest loans, and microfinance opportunities not only enable individuals to create businesses but also strengthen the economic fabric of the community. The Church, as an institution, plays an integral role in guiding community members toward these resources, encouraging entrepreneurship that aligns with the values and needs of the congregation.

Moreover, these partnerships extend beyond financial support, often involving mentorship and networking opportunities that allow aspiring entrepreneurs to learn from experienced professionals. By supporting businesses that prioritize community welfare, the Church actively contributes to a cycle of economic growth, reinforcing its role as a stronghold of hope and stability within the community.

Policy Advocacy for Economic Justice

While direct support through educational programs and financial partnerships is crucial, the Black Church also serves as a powerful advocate for systemic economic justice. By engaging in policy advocacy, the Church addresses the root causes of economic inequality, championing initiatives that promote fair wages, affordable housing, and access to healthcare. This advocacy is not just a social responsibility but a spiritual mandate, as the Church's teachings emphasize compassion, equity, and justice. Advocating for fair wages and affordable housing reflects the Black Church's enduring commitment to economic justice, uniting its spiritual mission with practical efforts to promote equity and improve community well-being.

As the Church steps into the role of policy advocate, it brings visibility to the economic disparities affecting Black communities, often participating in coalitions that press for legislative changes. This approach empowers the Church to extend its influence beyond the immediate needs of its congregation, advocating for a society where economic stability and dignity are accessible to all. Policy initiatives addressing housing affordability, healthcare equity, and income equality are essential components of this mission, with the Church acting as both a moral guide and an active participant in the fight for economic rights.

Through this advocacy, the Black Church reaffirms its role as an agent of change, committed to dismantling structural barriers that hinder economic progress within marginalized communities. The Church's advocacy for policies that uplift the economically disadvantaged amplifies its spiritual call to justice, reminding congregants and policymakers alike that economic empowerment is a vital aspect of faith. This vision is echoed by Lincoln and Mamiya (1990), who view the Church's influence in policy as a key mechanism for achieving long-term economic justice and community resilience.

Renewing the Church's Commitment to Social Justice and Advocacy

The Black Church has historically served as the moral compass and voice of advocacy within the Black community, embodying a prophetic tradition that champions justice and equity. As society continues to grapple with longstanding and emerging social injustices, this role remains as vital as ever. Today, the Church must deepen its engagement, addressing a spectrum of issues that profoundly impact Black communities, from racial discrimination and healthcare disparities to educational inequities and mass incarceration. By amplifying marginalized voices and providing both practical and spiritual support, the Black Church continues its legacy as an agent of transformation.

Addressing Contemporary Social Issues

The Black Church's prophetic tradition has long propelled it to the forefront of social justice movements, from the Civil Rights Movement of the 1960s to present-day initiatives against systemic inequality. This legacy requires the Church to continually address issues that disproportionately affect Black communities, acting as both advocate and support system. For generations, the Black Church has led the struggle for social justice by mobilizing faith and collective action to challenge systems of inequality and to advocate for fair access to education, healthcare, and opportunity within Black communities. In this way, the Church's mission extends beyond the spiritual, encompassing a commitment to social reform and systemic justice.

In the face of modern racial injustice, the Black Church continues to be a pivotal force, grounded in the legacy of leaders who have fought for dignity and equity. In addressing contemporary racial inequities, the Black Church continues to model faithful engagement in public life, translating its spiritual convictions into advocacy, service, and leadership that advance justice and affirm the God-given worth of every person. The Church's response to issues like mass incarceration and racial profiling reinforces its commitment to challenging structures of oppression. By advocating for policy reforms and providing resources such as legal aid and reentry programs, the Church seeks to dismantle barriers that marginalize and criminalize Black individuals.

Healthcare disparities also persist as significant challenges, affecting physical and mental health within Black communities. The Black Church's response has been multifaceted, including advocacy for equitable healthcare policies, community health education, and direct services like health screenings and counseling (Dorrien, 2023). By addressing healthcare inequities, the Church upholds its mission to nurture the well-being of its members, recognizing that physical health is integral to spiritual and communal strength.

In the realm of education, the Church's advocacy for accessible, quality education resonates with its foundational commitment to uplift future generations. The Church provides tutoring programs, college preparatory resources, and scholarship opportunities that help bridge the educational gaps faced by Black youth. The Church's mission extends to education as a foundational calling, championing quality learning environments that empower, affirm, and uplift Black children and young adults within their communities. In supporting educational access, the Church ensures that its younger members have the tools needed to achieve their potential, empowering them to contribute meaningfully to their communities.

Engaging in Community-Based Social Services

Beyond advocacy, the Black Church also embodies its commitment to social justice through community-based services, offering tangible support to address immediate and systemic needs. Community service is not merely an extension of the Church's work; it is central to its mission. Community service is integral to the Church's mission. Providing food, shelter, and mental health support are essential resources that uplift and stabilize the lives of congregants and neighbors alike. These services reflect the Church's dedication to holistic care, addressing physical, emotional, and spiritual needs.

Food banks, shelters, and mental health support have become essential services that many Black churches offer, particularly in response to rising poverty rates and mental health crises within their communities. By establishing these services, the Church not only provides for its members but also strengthens its surrounding neighborhoods. The creation of food banks and community support programs within Black churches reflects a practical commitment to meeting immediate needs while simultaneously working to confront and reduce systemic poverty. In this way, the Church becomes a stronghold of stability and compassion, ensuring that no member of the community is left without support.

Furthermore, the Church's mental health programs reflect its understanding of the need for comprehensive care. Recognizing that spiritual support alone cannot address all struggles, many Black churches now offer counseling services, workshops on mental health awareness, and spaces for open discussion on mental well-being (Mattis & Grayman-Simpson, 2013). By providing these resources, the Church acknowledges the importance of mental health within its holistic approach to ministry.

Educational programs also play a critical role in the Church's social services, from after-school tutoring to college prep resources, which help bridge gaps in academic support for Black youth. Educational programs such as after-school tutoring and college preparation initiatives have become essential components of the Church's outreach, providing critical academic support and helping to close educational gaps within the community. These initiatives are not merely charitable acts but are aligned with the Church's mission of empowerment, equipping the community's youth with tools to succeed.

Partnering With Social Justice Organizations

Unity is where the power of the Black Church lies, and that power comes into play with its partnerships with organizations devoted to social justice. When the Black Church joins forces with groups seeking to achieve racial justice, economic power, and equity in healthcare, the dynamic that generates real change becomes even more potent. These organizations create a network that, together with the Black Church, forms the vanguard of a movement that achieves significant milestones.

As these collaborations expand, so does the Church's scope and influence. It engages directly with local and national groups to tackle some of society's most stubborn problems, like pushing back against efforts to suppress voting, ensuring that housing is free from discrimination, and working for environmental justice. These are not quick fixes; they're deeply embedded issues that require collective determination to dismantle. The Church comes prepared, leveraging its size and resources with a strategic focus to make waves in advocacy and policy. Together with its coalition of allies, it's building a unified front that amplifies its influence and pressure for positive change.

These alliances are impactful not only because they bring together numerous organizations but because, collectively, these organizations and their resources enable the Church to address the root causes of inequality directly. Each group brings unique expertise, and when these are combined with the Church's resources and initiatives, they deliver significant benefits to communities. As Mohamed et al. (2021) noted, "I don't want to overstate the decline of the Black minister, but the civil rights movement had a certain kind of face to it. The vanguard was religious leaders, and that has changed" (p. 141). In response to the shift identified by Mohamed et al., collaborative efforts are recommended to help the Church engage in policy advocacy that positively impacts Black communities and, by extension, enhances the quality of life for all.

This strategy underlines the importance of strategic partnerships among religious institutions, policymakers, and community organizations to promote equitable policies and build environments that support social justice and community well-being.

Beyond the practical benefits, these partnerships give the Church significant social capital, adding a new dimension to its role in public life. Working with a range of organizations focused on economic justice, healthcare, and racial equity, the Church has become a model for inclusive activism. It's a strategy that wins over critics and bolsters the Church's voice in public policy debates. But make no mistake—these collaborations aren't just for appearances. They're about creating real, lasting change, driving forward a vision of justice and equity that benefits everyone involved.

Education and Cultural Development as Sacred Missions

The Black Church has long been a cornerstone of both spiritual and intellectual empowerment in the African American community. It's a hub where faith, education, and culture converge to uplift individuals and fortify the community. From the establishment of schools during Reconstruction to modern-day scholarship programs and cultural initiatives, the Church has consistently prioritized learning as a pathway to liberation. As Wilmore (1998) highlights, the Black Church has functioned as a formative institution, shaping the minds and spirits of those who look to it for guidance.

By preserving cultural memory and fostering education, the Black Church prepares its members to navigate societal challenges with confidence. This dual mission of nurturing both the spirit and the intellect ensures that the Church remains a vital force, inspiring individuals to embrace their identity and strive for progress in every sphere of life.

The Church's Role in Educational Empowerment

Throughout history, the Black Church has functioned as a vital educational institution, particularly during times when formal educational opportunities for African Americans were limited or inaccessible. Beyond spiritual teachings, the Church has taken on the responsibility of promoting literacy, providing life skills training, and fostering academic achievement. This commitment is reflected in programs such as after-school tutoring, scholarships, and mentorship initiatives that are grounded in the Church's belief that education is a sacred pathway to freedom and empowerment (Allen, 2023).

Educational empowerment is woven into the fabric of the Black Church's mission. Through partnerships with schools, scholarship funds, and structured educational programs, the Church instills a collective belief in the life-altering power of knowledge. The Church functions as an informal school, providing guidance and resources that go beyond spiritual teaching to include practical skills, personal development, and opportunities that help cultivate purposeful and productive lives. Such efforts symbolize the community's shared investment in the youth's potential and future, emphasizing that true liberation encompasses both spiritual and intellectual freedom.

Education within the Church is not only an individual journey but a communal responsibility. Scholarship programs and tutoring initiatives reflect the Church's dedication to nurturing young minds, cultivating a future generation that is both well-prepared and grounded in the values of faith. In these ways, the Church serves as a sanctuary for learning, a place where academic and spiritual growth intertwine. This commitment is a testament to the Church's recognition that to fulfill its sacred mission, it must prepare individuals to navigate a complex world with wisdom, integrity, and purpose (Brewer & Williams, 2019).

Promoting Cultural Heritage and History Preservation

The Black Church also stands as a preserver of cultural heritage, actively promoting the history and resilience of the African American experience. Through storytelling, music, and communal events, the Church cultivates a rich cultural memory that honors the struggles and achievements of past generations. This cultural preservation is essential for grounding the community in a collective identity, fostering a sense of pride and unity among its members.

Programs focused on heritage and history preservation are integral to the Church's role as a cultural guardian. These initiatives celebrate African American history through events like Black History Month services, historical reenactments, and heritage festivals. The Church becomes a living repository for the stories of resilience, community, and strength, a guardian of Black history that passes on the legacy of those who came before. By upholding traditions and celebrating heritage, the Church serves as both a bridge to the past and a foundation for the future.

Intellectual Development as Worship

In the Black Church, the pursuit of knowledge is seen as a sacred act, a way of honoring both God and oneself. Intellectual growth is not separate from spiritual devotion; rather, it is viewed as an essential component of a faithful life. The Church promotes critical thinking, self-awareness, and social consciousness as parts of its mission to develop individuals who are equipped to contribute meaningfully to both the Church and the broader society.

This commitment to intellectual development as an act of worship aligns with a longstanding tradition in Black theology that sees knowledge as a pathway to understanding God's world and one's place within it. Everett (2012) describes the Black Church's emphasis on intellectual resilience as a reflection of its mission to cultivate not only spiritual devotion but also a profound sense of purpose and social responsibility. For the Church, fostering intellectual growth in its members is an acknowledgment that worship is enriched by knowledge, and that each person's potential is maximized through the pursuit of wisdom and understanding.

Moreover, by encouraging critical thinking, the Church empowers its members to become advocates for justice and agents of change. This intellectual rigor reinforces the Church's prophetic mission, equipping individuals with the knowledge to question, challenge, and transform societal structures that perpetuate inequality. The Church, therefore, is not merely a place of spiritual guidance but a forum for intellectual exploration and social critique, where learning is valued as a form of devotion to both God and community.

In this way, intellectual development within the Church serves as both a spiritual and social call to action. As congregants deepen their understanding of their faith, they are simultaneously inspired to act on their beliefs, to become informed leaders who embody the Church's commitment to justice and transformation. This holistic approach to worship and learning ensures that the Church remains a dynamic and forward-thinking institution, capable of addressing the complex issues faced by its community.

Cultivating Knowledge, Identity, and Action

The Black Church's commitment to education and cultural preservation reflects its broader mission: equipping its community with the tools to navigate a complex world while remaining deeply rooted in heritage. This mission goes beyond maintaining traditions; it's about creating pathways for empowerment that blend spiritual guidance with tangible action. The Church doesn't merely preserve history; it actively transforms it into a living resource, inspiring individuals to forge new futures informed by the lessons of the past. This engagement manifests in initiatives such as scholarship programs, leadership development, and cultural storytelling that affirm identity while addressing pressing contemporary challenges like economic inequity and social justice.

The sacred mission of the Black Church is not confined to spiritual salvation; it's about fostering a resilient and forward-thinking community that embodies the full spectrum of faith, intellect, and cultural pride. By blending education with empowerment, the Church provides a springboard for individuals to lead lives of purpose, advocacy, and transformation. In this way, the

Black Church remains not only a sanctuary of hope but also an engine for progress, shaping the future while honoring its rich legacy.

Mentorship and Training: Preparing Future Leaders for a Changing Church

Mentorship within the Black Church is more than a tradition—it is a sacred responsibility that ensures the Church remains relevant across generations. By nurturing future pastors and leaders, the Church preserves its mission of faith, cultural affirmation, and social justice, equipping the next generation to address the unique challenges of their time. This process is not just about passing down knowledge; it's about fostering a dynamic dialogue where emerging leaders bring fresh perspectives while drawing from the wisdom of their predecessors.

The role of mentorship is transformative, creating a foundation of support and guidance for young pastors who will shepherd congregations in an ever-changing world. Leadership demands courage and clarity to engage with the world's complexities. Mentorship within the Black Church prepares leaders to embody these traits, ensuring they are not only spiritually equipped but also socially conscious and prepared to address contemporary issues like economic inequality, mental health, and systemic injustice.

This commitment to mentorship reflects the Church's larger mission: to cultivate leaders who carry forward its values while reimagining how those values are expressed in modern contexts. By investing in mentorship and leadership training, the Black Church reinforces its role as a guiding force for both spiritual and social transformation, ensuring that its legacy of faith and action endures through the hands of capable, visionary leaders.

Preparing Future Leaders Through Mentorship

In the Black Church, mentorship is not just a process of teaching; it is a sacred covenant between elder pastors and young ministers, reflecting the profound duty of passing down values, traditions, and hard-won insights. Mentorship is viewed as the intentional passing down of faith and wisdom, serving as a spiritual act of preservation through which experienced leaders nurture the next generation. The elder mentors do not merely instruct; they nurture the young leaders to embody both the values and the prophetic voice that has historically set the Black Church apart.

This process of mentorship is transformative. In youth councils, elder-led Bible studies, and cross-generational worship sessions, young pastors are shown the depth of their heritage. McIntosh and Curry (2020) emphasize that mentorship binds the elder generation's lived experiences to the future leaders' fresh perspectives, creating a Church rooted in both history and hope. Through these interactions, young leaders gain an understanding of the historical contexts that shaped the Church's mission, and they develop a respect for the courage that allowed the Church to endure and thrive through countless social, political, and economic challenges.

Mentorship, therefore, is also a preparation for resilience. In this sacred exchange, young leaders learn how to navigate both the spiritual and practical dimensions of leadership. They gain the courage to speak truth to power, the compassion to minister to those in need, and the foresight to lead their congregations through challenging times. Through the careful guidance of seasoned mentors, emerging leaders are encouraged to cultivate patience, empathy, and a commitment to justice, which are critical attributes for those who will lead their congregations through times of social change.

Mentorship within the Black Church is rooted in accountability and service, ensuring that future leaders uphold the Church's mission of community well-being, justice, and advocacy. Dr. Robert Gaines II (2010) highlights that mentorship is more than teaching. Mentorship is a relational commitment to nurture leaders who will faithfully steward the Church's values and address the needs of their congregations with compassion and strength. This process not only equips mentees with the knowledge and skills necessary for leadership but also instills a deep sense of responsibility to their community and the broader mission of the Church.

The mentor-mentee relationship is profoundly sacred, symbolizing a covenant to honor the Church's legacy while responding to the evolving challenges of each era. This bond is not transactional but transformational, fostering a shared vision of leadership that balances reverence for tradition with an openness to new ideas. By cultivating leaders who embody both integrity and innovation, mentorship ensures that the Church remains a steadfast force for spiritual and social empowerment across generations.

The Role of Black Theological Institutions

Black theological institutions serve as vital pillars in preparing the next generation of leaders by providing a rigorous education that is steeped in both theological study and social relevance. Unlike mainstream seminaries, these institutions foster a unique understanding of the Church's mission, one that integrates both the spiritual formation of individuals and the advancement of social justice. Theological schools serve as sanctuaries of cultural pride, where students are not only trained in doctrine but are also grounded in the lived experiences, struggles, and victories of their communities.

For future pastors, the training offered by Black theological institutions is invaluable. These institutions provide them with the intellectual and spiritual tools needed to navigate both the sacred texts and the social realities facing their congregations. Seminaries provide more than theological instruction; they cultivate the courage, resilience, and spiritual discernment needed to meet the complex challenges of ministry and public life. This dual mission reflects the Black Church's longstanding commitment to equip leaders who can speak to the complexities of Black life in America.

The role of theological education is also to instill a sense of historical continuity and respect for tradition. For many students, the experience of attending a Black theological institution is deeply transforming, as they gain a profound appreciation for the Black Church's legacy of advocacy, resistance, and spiritual leadership. These schools emphasize that theological knowledge alone is insufficient for effective ministry; it must be coupled with an understanding of the systemic issues that affect Black communities. Leaders are encouraged to view their pastoral roles as extensions of the Church's mission to advocate for justice and equality, ensuring that their ministries remain relevant to the social issues of the day.

In this sense, Black theological institutions act as stewards of the Church's prophetic voice. They remind future leaders that the Church is not only a spiritual sanctuary but also a beacon of hope and a defender of justice. Students are taught that their pastoral duties extend beyond the pulpit to the streets, courts, and schools, where their voices and actions can make tangible differences. This form of education equips pastors to integrate the Church's spiritual mission with active social engagement and prepare them to lead effectively and bridge divides within their congregations and communities.

Through theological education, future leaders gain not only an understanding of their faith but also a sense of responsibility for their communities. They are taught to lead with humility, wisdom, and a commitment to justice, ensuring that the Black Church remains a source of strength and advocacy in times of social unrest.

Leadership as a Sacred Responsibility

Leadership within the Black Church is seen as a sacred responsibility that demands both humility and a commitment to serve others selflessly. Unlike secular leadership roles, which may prioritize individual achievement, leadership in the Black Church is rooted in a communal ethic. Leaders are called to serve as both spiritual guides and advocates for justice, embodying the Church's mission in their daily actions and decisions. This sacred duty, passed down through generations, binds each pastor to a legacy of service, advocacy, and resilience.

In mentorship, emerging leaders are shown that true leadership is not about authority or status, but about embodying the values of the Church and using one's influence to uplift others. Mentorship within the Black Church extends beyond offering guidance; it focuses on shaping leaders who deeply understand, live out, and advance the Church's mission in both faith and action. This understanding transforms leadership into a calling, a commitment to serve with integrity, empathy, and a dedication to justice.

Young leaders learn from their mentors that the Black Church's role extends beyond the pulpit. They are trained to be advocates for their congregants, recognizing that spiritual leadership involves addressing the material and social realities that shape their lives. By instilling a sense of accountability, mentorship prepares pastors to use their influence for the betterment of their communities, challenging societal injustices and advocating for policies that promote equality and equity.

Education as a Communal Journey

The Black Church has long held the conviction that education is not merely an individual pursuit, but a communal journey that benefits everyone. As I have noted, "The pursuit of knowledge is not only my personal journey but a communal one. The entire community rises when one of us achieves intellectual freedom" (Richardson, 2020). These words underscore a core principle of the Black Church: education is a shared endeavor that strengthens the fabric of the entire community. This communal perspective on education transforms each academic milestone into a collective triumph, reinforcing the interconnectedness of individual success and community resilience.

This communal approach to education stems from a deep-seated belief that each individual's intellectual growth uplifts not only their family but the community as a whole. Educating a single child has the power to strengthen an entire family and, ultimately, the wider community, transforming personal achievement into a shared victory that uplifts all. The Church has embraced this philosophy by establishing and supporting institutions of learning that serve the community and nurture future generations of leaders.

Preserving Culture Through Education

Our role in education extends beyond the confines of Sunday worship. The Black Church functions as a repository of Black culture, where our shared stories, music, and traditions are passed down and celebrated. The Church's commitment to education also involves fostering an environment where Black identity is both preserved and developed. This commitment to cultural education is vital in the face of societal pressures that seek to distort or erase the contributions of Black people. Through our educational programs, we resist erasure by ensuring that every generation understands its roots, triumphs, and struggles. Cone and Wilmore (1979) wrote, "The African brand of Christianity emphasized the solidarity of past, present, and future, and reverence for ancestors, which secured the continuity and resilience of each community." We thus remain keepers of our history and nurturers of our future, preserving cultural continuity in the face of systemic oppression.

Knowledge as Sacred Power

The intellectual journey encouraged within the Black Church is both individual and collective. Within the tradition of the Black Church, intellectual development is inseparably linked with spiritual maturity, each reinforcing the other to cultivate a balanced and faithful life. This intertwining of knowledge and faith underscores the Church's belief that education serves as a spiritual foundation for social empowerment and justice. Through both theological and secular education, the Black Church fosters values of resilience, justice, and community in future generations.

Our intellectual mission holds that knowledge is power—but not power for the sake of dominance. Rather, knowledge is revered as a tool of liberation and a form of worship that brings us closer to God. It is a pathway through which we fulfill our sacred duties, offering each congregant the means to live a life of purpose, informed by both intellect and faith. The intellectual growth fostered by the Black Church enables individuals to transcend societal limitations, reclaiming dignity and humanity in a world that often seeks to deny them.

Through the collective pursuit of knowledge, we make God's presence known in every sphere of our lives—educational, spiritual, and social. This pursuit is not a mere academic exercise; it is an act of worship, a reclaiming of our God-given dignity, and a manifestation of our covenant with God. The intellectual growth fostered within the Black Church guides us toward a future where we can thrive as a community united by both faith and knowledge.

The Living Impact of the Black Church

Looking ahead, the mission of the Black Church is not merely to safeguard traditions but to carry them forward into new contexts. This requires cultivating spaces where education, inquiry, and innovation thrive alongside faith. It means creating opportunities for every member of the community to contribute their unique gifts and talents, ensuring the Church remains a source of strength, hope, and transformation. As we strive to empower future generations, we honor the sacred legacy of the Church while equipping it to meet the needs of an evolving world.

The Black Church's work is not only about preservation but renewal—a continuous effort to challenge injustices, uplift the marginalized, and foster resilience within the community. This mission reflects a deep calling to embody God's justice and love in action. By embracing this dual role as both a sanctuary and a platform for empowerment, the Black Church can continue to inspire hope, lead with purpose, and remain a guiding light for generations to come.

The Ark of the Covenant: A Biblical Blueprint for Future Leadership

The biblical instructions for carrying the Ark of the Covenant provide a compelling metaphor for how the Black Church must prepare its future leaders. In Numbers, God's specific directives for the Levites—to carry the Ark with poles, treating it with utmost reverence—signify the sacred responsibility of leadership (*New King James Version*, 1982, Numbers 4:15, 7:9). This imagery reminds us that leadership within the Church requires a foundation of respect, dedication, and communal effort, much like the shared responsibility of the Levites. It also underscores that the Church's mission is not an individual calling but a collective covenant sustained through intergenerational mentorship, theological training, and cultural grounding (McCalla, 2005).

Preparing future pastors requires more than a theological education; it demands that they be steeped in the history, culture, and lived realities of the Black community. Mentorship serves as a sacred bridge, transferring wisdom from one generation to the next. Seasoned leaders guide emerging pastors through the complexities of addressing spiritual needs, economic disparities, and systemic injustice, ensuring they are equipped to uphold the Church's mission in every context (W. Spencer, 2022). This ongoing exchange between generations sustains the vitality of the Black Church where leadership remains rooted in tradition while embracing innovation to meet the needs of a changing world.

Black theological institutions and seminaries stand as modern "Levitical training grounds," where future leaders receive both intellectual rigor and spiritual formation. These spaces provide a critical foundation, equipping pastors to navigate the intersection of faith, justice, and cultural preservation. In these institutions, leaders learn how to carry the Church's mission with a balance of prophetic vision and pastoral care, addressing contemporary issues like economic inequity, mental health, and community empowerment (Buffel, 2017). This preparation instills a sense of purpose, ensuring that each leader approaches their role with reverence, humility, and a deep commitment to justice.

Carrying the Covenant Forward

The Ark of the Covenant, as a symbol of God's presence and promises, represents a sacred trust that requires both care and action. Similarly, the leaders of the Black Church are entrusted with safeguarding its mission while leading their congregations toward growth and transformation. This is not merely about maintaining tradition; it is about expanding the Church's impact to meet the challenges of a rapidly evolving world.

Future pastors and leaders must embrace their role as bearers of God's presence, tasked with guiding their communities through both spiritual and societal struggles. By grounding their leadership in faith, justice, and resilience, they ensure that the Black Church remains a dynamic force for liberation, unity, and hope.

As we look to the future, our covenant with God compels us to honor the sacred mission of the Church while empowering new generations to reimagine its possibilities. The Ark is not a relic of the past; it is a living testament to God's enduring promises. By investing in mentorship, education, and the cultivation of prophetic leadership, the Black Church will continue to thrive as a vessel of faith, justice, and transformation for generations to come.

A Future and a Hope

The Rev. Dr. Martin Luther King Jr.'s poignant question, posed in the very title of his 1967 work *Where Do We Go From Here: Chaos or Community?*, resonates deeply as the Church looks to the future. The answer lies in the Church's steadfast commitment to be both a bastion of hope and a builder of community. This is not merely a spiritual calling but a communal one, requiring the collective effort of leaders, congregants, and supporters to sustain and expand the Church's mission.

The Black Church is more than a preserver of traditions; it is an innovator, a mentor, and a visionary institution that bridges the past and future. As it continues to embrace its role as a vessel of divine purpose, the Church must remain vigilant in raising leaders who can adapt modern perspectives to address contemporary issues meaningfully. Through education, mentorship, and activism, the Black Church will ensure its enduring mission inspires and empowers future generations.

This sacred promise is one we all share. As we move forward, let us commit ourselves to carrying the Church's legacy into the future with reverence and boldness. The Ark of the Covenant is not merely a relic of ancient scripture—it is a living testament to God's enduring promise, carried forward in the hearts, actions, and faith of His people. Together, let us ensure the Black Church thrives as a vessel of purpose, progress, and unyielding hope, embodying the sacred promise of a more just and empowered future.

References

Allen, S. E. (2023). Is the Black Church dead?: Religious resilience and the contemporary functions of Black Christianity. *Religions, 14*(460), 1–21.

Avent, J. R., & Cashwell, C. S. (2015). The Black Church: Theology and implications for counseling African Americans. *The Professional Counselor, 5*(1), 81–90.

Barber, K. H. (2015). Whither shall we go? The past and present of Black churches and the public sphere. *Religions 6*(1), 245–265. https://doi.org/10.3390/rel6010245

Barber, W. J., & Wilson-Hartgrove, J. (2016). *The third reconstruction: Moral Mondays, fusion politics, and the rise of a new justice movement.* Beacon Press.

Barnes, S. L. (2005). Black Church culture and community action. *Social Forces, 84*(2), 967–994.

Barnes, S. L. (2023). J-setting and Jesus: Spirituality and sanctuary. In *From Jesus to J-setting: Religious and sexual fluidity among young Black people* (pp. 1–28). University of Georgia Press.

Blank, M. B., Mahmood, M., Fox, J. C., & Guterbock, T. (2002). Alternative mental health services: The role of the Black Church in the South. *American Journal of Public Health, 92*(10), 1668–1672.

Blight, D. W. (2018). *Frederick Douglass: Prophet of freedom.* Simon & Schuster.

Bonhoeffer, D. (1949). *The cost of discipleship.* SCM Press.

Brewer, L. C., & Williams, D. R. (2019). We've come this far by faith: The role of the Black Church in public health. *American Journal of Public Health, 109*(3), 385–386.

Brown, R. E. (1994). *An introduction to New Testament Christology.* Paulist Press.

Buffel, O. A. (2017). Black theology and the Black experience in the midst of pain and suffering amidst poverty. *Scriptura, 116*(1), 1–14.

Campbell, H. A., & Tsuria, R. (2021). *Digital religion: Understanding religious practice in digital media.* Routledge.

Chandler, D. J. (2017). African American spirituality: Through another lens. *Journal of Spiritual Formation & Soul Care, 10*(2), 159–181.

Cone, J. H. (1975). *God of the oppressed.* Orbis Books.

Cone, J. H. (1997). *Black theology and Black power.* Orbis Books.

Cone, J. H., & Wilmore, G. S. (Eds.). (1979). *Black theology: A documentary history, volume one: 1966–1979.* Orbis Books.

Daughtry, L. (2021, April 8). *Of impact, of influence: The Black Church in contemporary American politics.* Berkley Center for Religion, Peace, & World Affairs. https://berkleycenter.georgetown.edu/responses/ of-impact-of-influence-the-black-church-in- contemporary-american-politics

Dempsey, K., Butler, S. K., & Gaither, L. (2016). Black churches and mental health professionals: Can this collaboration work? *Journal of Black Studies, 47*(1), 73–87.

Dorrien, G. (2023). The Gospel is a social gospel. *Commonweal, 150*(5), 14–16.

Douglas, K. B. (1999). *Sexuality and the Black Church: A womanist perspective.* Orbis Books.

Du Bois, W. E. B. (1903). *The souls of Black folk.* A.C. McClurg & Co.

Everett, D. L. (2012). *A future horizon for a prophetic tradition: A missional, hermeneutical, and pastoral leadership approach to education and Black Church civic engagement.* (Doctoral dissertation). Luther Seminary.

Fisher, E. J. (2023). *The Reverend Albert Cleage Jr. and the Black Prophetic Tradition: A reintroduction of The Black Messiah.* Lexington Books/Fortress Academic.

Gaines, R. W. (2010). Looking back, moving forward: How the civil rights era church can guide the modern Black Church in improving Black student achievement. *The Journal of Negro Education, 79*(3), 366–379.

Glaude, E. S. (2020). *Begin again: James Baldwin's America and its urgent lessons for our own.* Crown.

Grigsby, D. (2021). The Black Church: A gift for all. *New Horizons, 5*(1), 9–17.

Higginbotham, E. B. (1993). *Righteous discontent: The women's movement in the Black Baptist Church, 1880–1920.* Harvard University Press.

Hunter, C. (2022). The African American church house: A phenomenological inquiry of an Afrocentric sacred space. *Religions, 13*(3), 246.

Hutchings, T. (2017). *Creating church online: Ritual, community, and new media.* Routledge.

King, M. L., Jr. (1962, September 12). [Speech given on the centennial anniversary of the Preliminary Emancipation Proclamation.] Park-Sheraton Hotel, New York City, NY, United States.

King, M. L., Jr. (1967a, April). Beyond Vietnam—A Time to Break Silence [Speech]. Riverside Church, New York City, NY, United States.

King, M. L., Jr. (1967b). *Where do we go from here: Chaos or community?* Harper & Row.

Mattis, J. S., & Grayman-Simpson, N. A. (2013). Faith and the sacred in African American life. In *APA handbook of psychology, religion, and spirituality* (Vol. 1, pp. 547–564). https://doi.org/10.1037/14045-030

May, H. G. (1936). The Ark: A miniature temple. *The American Journal of Semitic Languages and Literatures, 52*(4), 215-234. https://www.jstor.org/stable/529185

McCalla, D. (2005). Black churches and voluntary action: Their social engagement with the wider society. *Black Theology: An International Journal, 3*(2), 137–175.

McGrath, A. (1996). *Christian theology: An introduction.* Wiley-Blackwell.

McIntosh, R., & Curry, K. (2020). The role of a Black Church—school partnership in supporting the educational achievement of African American students. *School Community Journal, 30*(1), 161–189.

Mohamed, B., Cox, K., Diamant, J., & Gecewicz, C. (2021). *Focus groups: A look at how Black Americans talk about "Black churches."* Pew Research Center. https://www.jstor.org/stable/resrep62898.4

Moltmann, J. (1967). *Theology of hope.* Harper & Row.

New King James Version. (1982). Thomas Nelson.

Pannenberg, W. (1991). *Systematic theology.* Eerdmans.

Pattillo-McCoy, M. (1998). Church culture as a strategy of action in the Black community. *American Sociological Review, 63*(6), 767–784.

Perkins, M. Y. (2019). The praxis of prophetic voice: Martin Luther King, Jr. and strategies for resistance. *Black Theology: An International Journal, 17*(3), 241–257.

Pinn, A. B. (2002). *The Black Church in the post-Civil Rights era.* Orbis Books.

Raboteau, A. J. (2004). *Slave religion: the "invisible institution" in the Antebellum South* (2nd ed.). Oxford University Press.

Ransby, B. (2018). *Making all Black lives matter: Reimagining freedom in the twenty-first century.* University of California Press.

Ray, S. F. (1967). *Journeying through a jungle.* National Baptist Publishing Board.

Richardson, W. F. (2006a). Emmanuel: God with us. In O. Cloud (Ed.), *Joy to the world: Inspirational Christmas messages from America's preachers* (pp. 263–269). Atria Books.

Richardson, W. F. (2006b). Joy to the world. In O. Cloud (Ed.), *Joy to the world: Inspirational Christmas messages from America's preachers* (pp. 3–10, 263–269). Atria Books.

Richardson, W. F. (2020). *Speaking truth to power: The role of the Black Church in social justice* [Speech audio recording]. Grace Baptist Sermons.

Richardson, W. F. (2021). *Pandemic lessons: Reimagining the Black Church in a digital era* [Speech audio recording]. Grace Baptist Sermons.

Richardson, W. F. (2022). *Anchoring hope: The role of the Black Church in changing times* [Speech audio recording]. Grace Baptist Sermons.

Sharpton, A. & Hunger, K. (2002). *Al on America*. Kensington Publishing Corp.

Smith, C., & Snell, P. (2009). *Souls in transition: The religious and spiritual lives of emerging adults*. Oxford University Press.

Spencer, W. F. (2022). The Black Church: A place of refuge–a place of prayer. *Masters Essay, 154*, 1–35.

Spurgeon, C. H. (1863). *The power of Aaron's rod* (Sermon No. 521). Delivered at the Metropolitan Tabernacle, Newington, July 26, 1863. Retrieved from https://www.spurgeongems.org

Spurgeon, C. H. (1889). *The Filling of Empty Vessels* (Sermon No. 2063). Delivered at the Metropolitan Tabernacle, Newington, intended for reading on Lord's Day, January 13, 1889. Retrieved from https://www.spurgeongems.org

Spurgeon, C. H. (1895). *The ark of his covenant* (Sermon no. 2427). Delivered at the Metropolitan Tabernacle, Newington, August 18, 1887. Published for reading on August 25, 1895. Retrieved from https://www.spurgeongems.org

Spurgeon, C. H. (1970). *The Oil and the Vessels* (Sermon No. 1467A). Written at Mentone. Retrieved from https://www.spurgeongems.org

Stott, J. (1986). *The cross of Christ.* InterVarsity Press.

Taylor, G. C. (1977). *How shall they preach.* Progressive Baptist Publishing House.

Taylor, J. (2020). The roots of the Black prophetic voice. *Christianity Today, 64*(6), 58–62.

Taylor, K. Y. (2016). *From #BlackLivesMatter to Black liberation.* Haymarket Books.

Taylor, N. M. (2023). *Brooding over Bloody Revenge: Enslaved Women's Lethal Resistance.* Cambridge University Press.

Thorsen, D. (2020). God with us. *What's true about Christianity?: An introduction to Christian faith and practice* (Vol. 1, pp. 91–96). Claremont Press.

Walker, W. T. (1979). *Somebody's calling my name.* Judson Press.

Walker, W. T. (1988). *Spirits that dwell in deep woods II: The prayer and praise hymns of the Black religious experience.* Martin Luther King Fellows Press.

West, C. (1982). *Prophesy deliverance!: An Afro-American revolutionary Christianity.* Westminster Press.

Wilkes, A. (2024). *Plenty good room: Co-creating an economy of enough for all.* Broadleaf Books.

Williams, D. S. (1993). *Sisters in the wilderness: The challenge of womanist God-talk.* Orbis Books.

Williams, J., Pressley, T., Jackson, M. S., & Barnett, T. (2019). Black megachurches and the provision of social services: An examination of regional differences in America. *Journal of Religion & Spirituality in Social Work, 38*(1), 1–19.

Williams, T. (2022). *Black church/white theology: How white evangelicalism controls the Black Church.* Church Digest Books.

Wilmore, G. S. (1983). *Black religion and Black radicalism: An interpretation of the religious history of Afro-American people* (2nd ed.). Orbis Books.

Wilmore, G. S. (1998). *Black religion and Black radicalism: An interpretation of the religious history of African Americans.* Orbis Books.

Zanfagna, C. (2017). *Holy hip hop in the City of Angels.* University of California Press.

Endorsements

Rev. Dr. Boise Kimber
President, National Baptist Convention, USA, Inc.

Dr. W. Franklyn Richardson's *Never Lost* is not just a book—it is a symphony of faith, fortitude, and purpose that resonates with the beating heart of the Black Church. As I turned its pages, I was struck by the profound wisdom of a man I have long admired, a mentor to many of us in ministry, and a guiding light in the struggle for justice. Richardson's reflections are not merely observations; they are the lived truths of a leader who has carried the weight of the Church's sacred calling through the storms of our time. His words remind us that the Black Church has always been more than a sanctuary—it is an ark of liberation, preserving the soul of our people and charting a course toward a more just and equitable world.

Never Lost reads as a personal letter to leaders like me because it urges us to remember that our sacred duty extends beyond the pulpit. Richardson masterfully reminds us that, while the Black Church is rooted in tradition, it must also be a force of innovation that boldly addresses the challenges of today with the same courage that carried us through the trials of the past. His vision of the Church as God's Ark of the Covenant stirs something deep within me—a call to lead with humility, strength, and an unwavering commitment to justice.

I commend this extraordinary work not just as a book but as a beacon for all who believe in the transformative power of faith. *Never Lost* is a gift to the Black Church and a challenge to us all to rise, to lead, and to never lose sight of the promises of God.

Bishop Lawrence Reddick III

Senior Bishop and Chief Executive Officer,
Christian Methodist Episcopal (CME) Church

Never Lost: The Black Church as God's Ark of the Covenant makes a striking statement in comparing the Black Church to the Ark of the Covenant for the biblical Israel. I am sure many biblical literalists will be slow to allow such a statement without strong opposition or, at the least, hesitancy. But we must acknowledge that original ideologies from leaders of the Black Church have usually been challenged and by people who do not understand the Black Church and its differences of theological understanding of God's salvation history—the story of God's redemptive relationships with and as understood by Black and other colored peoples. The dominant theological messages taught in seminaries across the world have been European in origin or nuance, and many want those messages to be the only ones that exist. Perhaps you can recall the Presidential campaign of 2008 when Barack Obama was under fire because his pastor, Dr. Jeremiah Wright, was a proponent of Black Liberation Theology— and the media voices found other clergy who would say that is/was no such thing. However, I remembered being taught about liberation theology from a Black and a South American lens in the predominantly White theology seminary I had attended a full 30 years before!

Before you read this book, it may help to consider the prominence of Richardson's endeavors and his impact in the world.

First, Rev. Dr. W. Franklyn Richardson graduated from Richmond's local historically Black college and university (HBCU), Virginia Union University, with a bachelor of arts degree; Yale Divinity School with a master of divinity; and United Theological Seminary with a doctor of ministry. He is a learned and lettered person.

Second, Richardson is in his 50th year as pastor of the Grace Baptist Church of Mount Vernon, New York, so there is longevity of leadership and relationships and "followship" in the church world he speaks about and to.

Third, Richardson is chair of three related but very differently focused organizations: the Conference of National Black Churches, the Board of Trustees of Virginia Union University, and the National Action Network (NAN).

The Conference of National Black Churches is an ecumenical organization of six denominations that are both national and international in scope. For 10 years, Richardson has guided the leaders of these six predominantly African American organizations by convening annual conferences for intellectual, spiritual, and justice-oriented cooperation and engagement among them. These denominations are the Church of God in Christ (COGIC), the largest Black Pentecostal denomination in America; two internationally focused Baptist denominations—the National Baptist Convention, USA, and the Progressive National Baptist Convention; and three internationally focused Methodist Episcopal denominations—the African Methodist Episcopal (AME) Church, the African Methodist Episcopal Zion (AME

Zion) Church, and the Christian Methodist Episcopal (CME) Church.

As chair of the Board of Trustees for his alma mater, Virginia Union University, Richardson engages daily with the latest literature of the world of religion and many other liberal arts disciplines. He also communicates and partners with philanthropic organizations and their visionaries to accomplish the results that keep academic institutions alive and flourishing.

Richardson's voice of leadership and ear for dialogue is distinctly present as he chairs the Board of NAN, the social justice organization more closely defined by the activities across the nation of its prominently voiced president, the Reverend Al Sharpton.

Notes for the Reader

Never Lost: The Black Church as God's Ark of the Covenant is organized into eight chapters: (1) The Black Church as God's Ark of the Covenant; (2) Emmanuel, God With Us: The Black Church and a New Testament Hope; (3) The Evolving Practices of the Black Church in the 21st Century; (4) Community and the Gathering of Ourselves Together; (5) Preserving Black Culture Through Sacred Traditions; (6) Hearing the Prophetic Voices; (7) Creating Sacred Space for Healing and Empowerment; and (8) The Future of the Black Church and Its Covenant.

These eight chapters form the structural presentation of Richardson's arguments in *Never Lost*. The Ark of the Covenant, he writes in Chapter 1, was God's way of saying to the Israelites as they journeyed that God "was close by, traveling alongside the Israelites no matter where life took them." He expands on the concept of God journeying with humanity in the section titled "The Black Church as a Spiritual Refuge":

> The Black Church has long been a place of safety and fortitude within the Black community.
>
> ...
>
> The Church's significance extended beyond the individual. It was—and is—a place of shared stories and collective memory. Each Sunday, the community gathered not just for worship but for affirmation of their identity and value. In this sacred space, each voice, each hymn reverberated with the power of ancestral fortitude. The Church has become a place where individuals could affirm their humanity and receive dignity often denied elsewhere.

In Chapter 2, he describes how this accompaniment by God is not only an Old Testament theological concept but a New Testament concept because of the Incarnation of Jesus "as one of us." In the section titled "As Us: Jesus's Humanity and the Church's Incarnational Mission," he writes:

> In becoming human, Jesus signified that God came "as us," fully embracing the human

experience in all its complexity. The Incarnation reveals a profound act of solidarity, where God enters the world not merely to observe but to participate, to feel, and to suffer alongside humanity.

Richardson discusses the many ways the Black Church has changed throughout its existence in the third chapter. The Black Church is a symbol that morphs over time as it confronts new circumstances and contexts, and yet it performs the same role of re-presenting God's oneness with God's people and God's mercies to carry God's people "through" new times, contexts, and circumstances. He uses the Grace Baptist Church of Mount Vernon as a case study on how the Black Church pivoted during the COVID-19 pandemic that affected the world at the beginning of the 2020s. The church encouraged new ways to engage and communicate with its members and found that the new ways had become permanent ways to "do church." This chapter can be inspirational to pastors and local church leaders who need a toolkit or how-to manual.

Chapter 4 stresses the necessity for community and gathering. It especially makes clear that community and gathering are important in light of lessons learned from the COVID-19 pandemic. The Church (including the Black Church) is called to gather and to strengthen each other in gathering. In the first paragraph, Richardson declares, "This call to gather is not merely about physical proximity; it reflects a broader mission of fostering solidarity, social identity, and empowerment." An example of this fostering solidarity and social identity and empowerment was in the leadership of the Black Church during the Civil Rights Movement. Another was in the leadership of the Black Church during the COVID-19 pandemic.

In the fifth chapter, "Preserving Black Culture through the Sacred Traditions," Richardson points to the role that is broader than religious. For him it is also sociological in passing down the traditions that have informed who Black people in the Diaspora have been and are. He states in the chapter's first paragraph:

> The Black Church is the long-serving guardian of Black cultural identity, acting as a steadfast steward in preserving essential elements of African American heritage that might otherwise dissipate within broader societal currents. This sacred space is where the legacies of resilience, resistance, and faith intersect, enabling Black individuals to celebrate, nurture, and pass down the traditions that have shaped their history. Sacred traditions such as gospel music, call-and-response preaching, and communal rituals remain central to this mission.

In the opening paragraph of Chapter 6, Richardson highlights the importance of the prophetic voice in Black Church leadership: "Prophetic leadership has long defined the Black Church. From Nat Turner and Dr. Martin Luther King Jr. to contemporary voices like Rev. Al Sharpton, the Church has consistently produced leaders who speak truth to power, champion justice, and spark social change."

Chapters 7 and 8 are oriented toward leaders of the Black Church itself, challenging us to give attention to the purpose and intentionality and life of this institution in God's redemptive story.

Chapter 7, "Creating Space for Healing and Empowerment," reminds Black Church custodians to always be vigilant about the principles of being inclusive and creative. In the section titled "The Black Church as a Physical Sanctuary," Richardson writes, "The Black Church is a place where every life is treasured, every story is sacred, and every soul is renewed by the power of God's presence." He addresses such issues as mental health, bonding through community support, and clergy training for these types of issues. In the last section of the chapter, "Embracing the Future: A Vision of Holistic Well-Being," he advocates for transforming the Church into "a space where emotional and psychological well-being are as valued as spiritual health."

In Chapter 8, Richardson emphasizes the importance of bridging generational gaps. "The future of the Black Church," Richardson writes, "relies significantly on cultivating robust intergenerational leadership." In addition, he challenges the Black Church to be inclusive in its presentations of womanist theology and of affirming the experiences of Black women (lay and clergy) in the Church. The Black Church must be inclusive of all aspects of social justice.

In a final word about what Richardson presents in the structure of *Never Lost*, I consider the references listed to be helpful for the reader who wishes to learn more about the Black Church as God's specially nuanced instrument for redemption history.

I am one of the church denominational leaders who work alongside Dr. Richardson in the Conference of National Black Churches. In my role as Senior Bishop and CEO of the Christian Methodist Episcopal Church, I believe *Never Lost* is a helpful tool for church women and church men, lay and clergy, who may not have the wide berth of creative influences of those who have journeyed to highly regarded seminaries or who frequent engaging conferences. Richardson's words provide a simplicity of expression for those who need to hear new ideas and to hear not only the idea but suggestions for implementation.

Finally, I commend this book to your reading (especially if you are not a part of the Black Church) so that you may continue to dialogue with the Black Church—its history, its ways, and its present conversations—and, hopefully, be better informed of its visions, purposes, and intentions in this era.

Bishop Adam Jefferson Richardson Jr.
Senior Bishop, Retired,
African Methodist Episcopal (AME) Church

Never Lost: The Black Church as God's Ark of the Covenant is the latest installment of Dr. W. Franklyn Richardson's literary contribution to the church and the world. For more than half a century, he's been preaching the Gospel in pulpits across the world.

In *Never Lost*, Richardson is historian, theologian, and prophet. His keen political insights, in tandem with his biblical knowledge, provide a unique perspective on the meaning of the Black Church historically and for its promise. The Ark of the Covenant, alleged to be lost, is rediscovered in the Black Church. Dr. Richardson makes a serious case for its redemptive leadership role.

I am pleased to endorse *Never Lost* as a source of inspiration and a contemporary witness to the power of God working through God's Church. Generations unborn must see it, too. Those who lead the Church must handle it with care and prayer. They must value it as sacred, as the agency of God's promises to future generations in the pursuit of faith, peace, and justice.

Bishop J. Drew Sheard
Presiding Bishop and Chief Apostle,
Church of God in Christ (COGIC), Inc.

Dr. W. Franklyn Richardson's *Never Lost* is a profound and stirring tribute to the perseverance, faith, and transformative power of the Black Church as God's Ark of the Covenant. In this pivotal work, Richardson weaves together historical truths, theological insights, and personal reflections to illuminate the Church's role as a vessel of divine promise and communal strength. As the shepherd of the Church of God in Christ, I am deeply moved by Richardson's ability to frame the Black Church as not just a house of worship but as a living testament to God's faithfulness in every season of trial and triumph.

Dr. Martin Luther King Jr. said, "Faith is taking the first step even when you don't see the whole staircase" (1962). This profound truth echoes throughout *Never Lost* as Richardson reveals how the Black Church has long been a beacon of hope and faith, guiding God's people through trials and triumphs even in the face of uncertainty. His reflections compel us to honor our legacy while embracing the urgency of our sacred mission in these rapidly changing times.

Never Lost is more than a book; it is a call to action for leaders, congregants, and communities to see the Black Church not only as a place of spiritual refuge but as a prophetic force for justice and transformation. Richardson's reflections resonate deeply with my own experiences in ministry, particularly his vision of the

Church as a "living Ark" that carries the hope, identity, and dignity of Black people forward into uncharted territory. His words challenge us to lead with courage, guided by an unshakable faith in God's promises.

For those of us who hold the sacred responsibility of leadership, this work serves as both a guide and a charge to ensure that the Black Church remains a beacon of light and hope for generations to come. I wholeheartedly recommend *Never Lost* to anyone seeking to understand the enduring power and purpose of the Black Church in the lives of God's people.

Bishop Darryl B. Starnes Sr.

Senior Bishop,
African Methodist Episcopal Zion (AME Zion) Church

W. Franklyn Richardson's *Never Lost: The Black Church as God's Ark of the Covenant* is a profound and stirring exploration of the enduring legacy of the Black Church. In this masterful work, Dr. Richardson not only celebrates the Church's pivotal role as a spiritual haven but also underscores its transformative power as a beacon of hope, justice, and cultural preservation. The metaphor of the Black Church as an "Ark of the Covenant" is both poignant and fitting, capturing its sacred mission to carry forward the faith, resilience, and heritage of the African American community. Through rich historical context and personal reflection, Richardson reminds us that the Black Church is more than a house of worship; it is a custodian of divine purpose, sustaining communities through centuries of trials and triumphs.

What makes this book particularly compelling is Richardson's call to action for today's church leaders and congregants. As he reflects on the challenges of the present—from systemic inequities to the shifting dynamics of faith in the digital age—he offers a visionary blueprint for renewal and adaptation. His insights are both inspiring and urgent as he calls on the Black Church to honor its legacy while embracing innovation and inclusivity. *Never Lost* is not just a tribute to the past; it is a summons to rise and meet the demands of the future with the same unwavering commitment to justice, love, and community that has always defined the Black Church. This is a must-read for anyone seeking to understand the spiritual and cultural heartbeat of the African American experience and the enduring power of faith in action.

Rev. Dr. Jacqueline A. Thompson
Second Vice President,
Progressive National Baptist Convention (PNBC)

Never Lost: The Black Church as God's Ark of Covenant is a powerful corporate testimony that affirms the transformational role of the Black Church in American history and in the life of Black people. As the Ark of the Covenant served as a symbol of God's promise, presence, and power for the nation of Israel, so has the Black Church served as the physical symbol of the liberating love and power of God for Black people.

Dr. W. Franklyn Richardson delivers an engaging exploration of the deep impact of the Black Church in the fight for justice and equity for all humanity. It is timely and accessible, offering laity, clergy, and scholars historical and theological insight into the institution that has sought to preserve the faith, identity, and connection of a people.

Acknowledging the challenges the Black Church faces, Richardson issues a clarion call to remain faithful to the "covenantal mission" while seeking to innovate in ways that meet the needs of our time.

This is a must-read for all those who love, serve, and have hope for the Black Church as the Ark of the Covenant for Black people in the future.

Rev. Dr. David R. Peoples
President,
Progressive National Baptist Convention (PNBC)

I have walked with the Black Church long enough to know the difference between a book that speaks about us and a book that speaks for us. *Never Lost* speaks for us. Dr. W. Franklyn Richardson carries the weight of generations on every page, yet his words are light enough to lift weary hearts. I felt that lift from the first chapter. He calls the Church God's Ark for our people, and that image sings. An ark preserves life in a flood. The Black Church has preserved our dignity through storms of slavery, Jim Crow, and today's rolling waves of voter suppression and economic disparity. Reading these chapters, I heard the steady hum of that preservation. I heard the prayers of mothers under night skies. I heard the march cadence of our fathers' feet.

I serve a denomination that was formed so Dr. Martin Luther King Jr. could have a spiritual home when other tables turned him away. We were forged in dissent but shaped by hope. Every civil rights gain in this land found Progressive Baptists praying out front or pushing from behind. We know liberation is not a theory; it is a lifestyle. When Richardson writes that the Black Church must be both sanctuary and sword, my spirit shouts in agreement. He is telling our story, but he is also telling us to keep writing new chapters.

The scholarship in *Never Lost* is solid, but scholarship alone does not kindle holy fire. What kindles fire is testimony. Richardson does not hide behind footnotes. He tells stories of brush arbors turned into towers of faith, of pews that became planning rooms, of live streams that now carry gospel light to phones and tablets on kitchen tables. He shows how tradition can walk on new legs without losing its soul. I saw my own convention in those pages, still young enough to innovate, still old enough to remember.

The structure of the book is straightforward. Richardson roots us in history, names today's trials without flinching, then points to a future that feels both brave and reachable. He never lets the reader drift into nostalgia. Instead, he offers strategy. He lays out digital evangelism, intergenerational mentorship, and mental health partnerships like stepping stones across troubled water. He does not scold younger seekers who claim to be spiritual but not religious. He invites them to climb into the ark and help steer it.

What moves me most is his unshaken conviction that God is with us, for us, as us, and coming back for us. Those words echo every sermon I ever preached about perseverance. They remind me of the sweet assurance that anchors our hope. I've got somebody who knows who I am. That same Somebody guided Harriet Tubman's lantern, tuned Mahalia Jackson's voice, and parted voting lines last November. That same Somebody breathes through these pages.

You are in the world, but you do not have to be of the world. This book proves the point. It stands in the world's marketplace but speaks the language of the faithful. It calls us to move beyond roadside charity, for, as Dr. Martin Luther King Jr. reminded us, "We are called to play the Good Samaritan on life's roadside, but that will be only an initial act. One day we must come to see that the whole Jericho Road must be transformed so that men and women will not be constantly beaten and robbed as they make their journey on life's highway" (1967a). Richardson's prose is pastoral, prophetic, and practical, all in one breath. The Church cannot afford either timidity or triumphalism. We must stand tall and bend low at the same time. This volume shows us how.

I recommend *Never Lost* to pastors, scholars, activists, and all pilgrims who still believe the Black Church is God's gift to a hurting world. Read it slowly. Study it in small groups. Let it prod your conscience and warm your soul. If you join the conversation it sparks, you will find yourself part of an unbroken procession that stretches from plantation hush arbors to virtual pulpits, carrying the ark of covenant hope. There is freedom here. If you want that peace, you can receive it.

Biography

W. FRANKLYN RICHARDSON is Senior Pastor of Grace Baptist Church in the City of Mount Vernon, New York, and Chairman of the Board at Virginia Union University, his alma mater. He also serves as the Chairman of the Board of the National Action Network and Chairman of the Board of the Conference of National Black Churches. Richardson earned his divinity degree from Yale University Divinity School and his Doctorate of Ministry as a Wyatt Tee Walker Fellow from the United Theological Seminary in Dayton, Ohio. Mentored by Dr. Sandy Ray (a close friend of Dr. Martin Luther King Jr.) and Dr. Wyatt Tee Walker (Dr. King's chief of staff), Richardson has received numerous honors and accolades. Notable distinctions include induction into The Rev. Dr. Martin Luther King Jr. Board of Preachers and the International Hall of Honor by Morehouse College in Atlanta, Georgia, and recipient of The Alumni Award for Distinction in Congregational Ministry from Yale University. Richardson is married to Inez Nunnally Richardson and lives in New York.

www.ingramcontent.com/pod-product-compliance
Lightning Source LLC
Chambersburg PA
CBHW011120090426
42742CB00019B/3383

9781685480301